.50

IMMU

D0877094

F. M. BURNET
UNIVERSITY OF MELBOURNE

IMMUNOLOGY, AGING, AND CANCER

Medical Aspects
of Mutation and Selection

W. H. FREEMAN AND COMPANY
San Francisco

Library of Congress Cataloging in Publication Data

Burnet, Frank Macfarlane, Sir, 1899–
    Immunology, aging, and cancer.

    Bibliography: p.
    Includes index.
    1. Immune response. 2. Aging. 3. Cancer—
Immunological aspects. I. Title.
QR186.B87   616.07′9   76–16166
ISBN 0–7167–0490–0
ISBN 0–7167–0489–7 pbk.

Printed in the United States of America   9 8 7 6 5 4 3 2 1

CONTENTS

PREFACE

WHEN I ACCEPTED the invitation from students at University of California, Irvine, to give the lectures printed here, I stipulated that I would talk only about what I was currently interested in. This may explain the apparent wide range of topics contained within a very short series. It will be found, however, that there is a common Darwinian theme running through them all, a theme that I believe could provide a useful stimulus toward a fuller understanding of cellular biology as it bears on medicine. I have tried to simplify the discussion as much as possible, and without doubt some of my simplifications will be superseded in the future, but I hope that, till then, they may aid understanding for those interested in the biological borderlands of medicine. The lectures were given at Irvine in April 1975, and, in modified form, at the University of Southampton Medical School in the following month.

May I express my appreciation to the students at Irvine for the opportunity to spend three pleasant weeks on their campus, and especially to my student hosts, Kit Campion and Ken Lehmann, for their friendship and solicitude for my well being.

F. M. Burnet

Melbourne, Victoria
March 1976

IMMUNOLOGY, AGING, AND CANCER

THE BASIS
OF
IMMUNOLOGY

MEDICINE IS A FAR older human interest than biology, and the whole of my formal training was medical, yet in this re-shaping of a series of lectures to undergraduates the reader will find much more concern with biology than with medicine. If the book has a central theme, I should like to think that it is a consistent attempt to apply a Darwinian approach to cellular processes within the body. This holds particularly for my approach to immunology in the first four chapters, but a similar evolutionary attitude pervades the later chapters as well.

In this first section I want to present a broad picture of immunity and immunology as an element in the process by which we and all other mammals survive. Survival is the business of evolution, and if we are to have a satisfying understanding of any life phenomenon bearing on survival, we must have some concept of how it evolved. Let us look first at the sort of phenomena on which immunology is based. The first immunological observations were probably made long ago, when people began to recognize that an individual who had recovered from smallpox was immune against a second attack. Because anyone who had recovered carried the scars of his experience on his face, the relation of immunity to the fact of past infection was very obvious. Out of that observation came the idea that immunity to smallpox might be acquired, without facial disfigurement, by artificial variolation, or by Edward Jenner's vaccination with cowpox. That was the central concept of human immunology from Jenner's time to the present, with effective immunization against polio and measles being the last two significant achievements.

Incidental to such work was the discovery that usually recovery from infectious disease was associated with the presence in the blood of antibody, a modified immunoglobulin, a protein that would combine specifically with the responsible microorganism, and so facilitate its destruction in the body. I shall have a lot to say about antibody, but I should make it clear at once that nowadays we realize we know much less about how antibodies function than we thought we did 20 years ago. Gone forever is the comfortable idea that immunology meant finding the microorganism that causes a disease, making a vaccine, and protecting the child against that sort of infection by the antibody which the vaccine stimulates the body to produce. There is much more to it than that.

Probably the next immune phenomenon to be recognized was discovered by surgeons, especially plastic surgeons. They could patch up a man's injuries in remarkable fashion by taking grafts of bone or skin from one part of the body and implanting them where they could replace defects. But a piece of skin from another person was rejected within two weeks.

A final example which will help to complete the range of immunological phenomena and allow me to define the essential basis of immunity is the Rh baby. It is not uncommon to find a family in which, after two normal babies, the third is born suffering severe destruction of its red blood cells and, unless it receives an exchange transfusion of suitable blood, may die. Such a situation arises only when the father is Rh positive and the mother Rh negative, i.e., he produces red cells carrying a certain Rh antigen D but the mother does not. The fetus receives half its chromosomes from each parent and can therefore sometimes differ from the mother in having the Rh antigen D on its red cells. If those red cells enter the mother's circulation, she can respond by antibody production against the Rh antigen D, especially if she had been rendered susceptible by a previous pregnancy of the same quality. If the mother develops a high enough concentration of antibody in her blood, enough may leak into the fetus toward the end of pregnancy to give rise to hemolytic disease.

Basically, immunology is concerned with how and why the body reacts actively against almost anything that is foreign, that is genetically different from its own substance. Sometimes, as in rejecting a skin graft, or in a mother's attack on her own infant's red cells, the difference may seem very slight indeed. In immunology we are seeking to understand how the body can recognize the difference between self and not-self, and ensure that, whereas not-self is destroyed or cast off, the body's own self-substance normally provokes no reaction. There are, however, exceptions that will turn out to be important. Well before immunologists began to recognize the difficulties of grafts from other individuals, embryologists found that they could graft a piece of embryonic skin from one chicken embryo to another with ease, and have the recipient hatch and grow up with, for example, a patch of black feathers amongst its own uniform white ones. Workers with insects, too, found that they could transfer glands from one specimen to another without their being rejected. In general, invertebrates show little ability to recognize fine differences, although they will reject tissues from more distant species. Subject to minor qualifications, it is correct to say that vertebrates have a much finer capacity to distinguish self from not-self than invertebrates, and that before a certain stage in embryonic development vertebrates too fail to make these fine distinctions. But, as I shall have to say repeatedly, it is important to recognize that all general statements in immunology are likely to need qualification sooner or later. Immunology is a soft-edged science, and physicists and mathematicians are neither comfortable nor successful when they dabble in its problems.

I think it will be already evident, in what I have said, how importantly I believe that immunology is linked with genetics. When we use the terms "foreign" or "not-self" about cells or tissues, we mean always "not genetically proper to the individual." Once the concept of protein synthesis being governed by the genetic information in deoxyribonucleic acid (DNA) had been formulated, and especially when the way in which the information was transcribed and translated had been worked out, it was evident to everyone that the specific antibody pattern of immunoglobulin was genetically determined. The clonal selection theory was the first attempt to work out the mechanism by which that could be possible.

Genetic information is expressed in the phenotype only after a lengthy process in which synthesis of protein, including immunoglobulin and antibody as well as all the enzymes and structural proteins of the cell, is only the beginning. The process by which the fertilized egg cell, the zygote, proliferates into a ball of cells and then molds itself into developing organs and supporting tissues is differentiation, the next great problem for theoretical biology. Like the rest of the body, the immune system is a product of differentiation, and we have only a superficial picture of its progress at the cellular level. It is convenient, however, to outline the current convention for naming the main stages. This is a purely provisional schema that is bound to undergo progressive modification, but if I set it out here it will be easier to develop the discussion.

The sequence, then, begins with the hematopoietic stem cell from which all the mobile cells of blood and lymph are thought to develop. From one line of descendants come the lymphocytes, divided into T cells and B cells. At a certain stage, lymphocytes of both groups develop specific receptors which allow them to respond to contact, for each cell, with one particular type of antigen. I find it convenient to follow William Dameshek and call these immunocytes. "T cells" are so called because in mice they develop only in the thymus, which is also the dominant, but perhaps not the only, source in other mammals and birds. The name "B cells" originally referred to origin of these cells in the bursa of Fabricius of chickens, but nowadays the group is defined by the active production of immunoglobulin easily recognized on the cell surface by immunofluorescence. The final, mature, postmitotic state of the B cell takes the form of the plasma cell, a specialized factory for rapid immunoglobulin production.

This is probably enough to remind you of the general outline of vertebrate, and particularly mammalian, immunology as an introduction to saying something about the probable ways in which the immune system evolved. The main problem, and perhaps the only one which has a chance of being resolved, is how the effective but not very versatile defense mechanisms of most or all invertebrates developed into the refined and flexible immune system of the higher vertebrates. There are two aspects of vertebrate immunology that are common to all types above the most primitive forms. The first is the ability to produce recognized antibody and the second is exemplified by the fact that a man, a chicken, or a goldfish can recognize—by rejecting it—the foreignness of a piece of skin from another individual of the same species. No antibody has been observed in any invertebrate, and although slow rejection of foreign tissue grafts has been described in earthworms it is much less rapid and effective than rejection in mammals and birds. There are still many problems to be solved about both these aspects of immunity, and much of what I have to say in later chapters will be concerned with them. In this preliminary outline it is probably best to start by looking broadly at the situation in invertebrates.

Just as much as mammals, all invertebrates must have an effective set of mechanisms to avoid microorganismal invasion. Every living organism is a potential source of nutrients for the ever-present microorganisms in its environment, and effective defense is essential. It is conventional to put most responsibility on the wandering mesenchymal cells present in most or all metazoa. These are phagocytic for any microorganisms or particles of damaged tissue and are doubtless of importance for defense. However, this merely pushes the problem one step farther back. The capacity of the phagocytic cell to recognize the microorganism as foreign, and to digest it without damage to its own constituents, is presumably just a specialized example of a general capacity of living cells that may remain beyond analysis at the molecular level for a very long time.

I find that the more insight one gains into detailed processes within and between cells, the more difficult it is even to conceive how the almost infinite number of processes that are going on manage to avoid serious interference with one another. At all levels there must be "recognition" that the situation is as it should be or that something is wrong and calls for some correcting response. I can recognize that situation in the chromosomal mechanism of *Escherichia coli* or any other cell, in the reaction of the cytoplasm of a phagocytic cell to an ingested particle, or in the immune system as a whole, and I am dubious whether we shall ever reach the stage of interpreting it in molecular terms. I suspect that we may always have to be content with the use of general terms like recognition, specific response, activation, toxic damage, and so forth, in the explanation of most immunological phenomena, and attempt a deeper study only in a few specially favorable situations.

With this modest objective, let us start with invertebrate reactions that show at least a capacity to differentiate between self and not-self. It is well known that a variety of colonial marine organisms will fail to fuse with a portion of any colony that is not genetically similar. At the interface a damaging interaction takes place and a clear line of demarcation develops. Theodor's analysis (1971) of this in *Gorgonia* assumes the existence of a bifunctional killer molecule in the tissues of each which is held inert by being specifically bound to a self-type inhibitor. When the killer molecule complex diffuses into the foreign tissue, it is liable to dissociate, and the absence of a specific inhibitor of the right type allows its toxic quality to be exercised. The essential feature in these organisms, and probably in all metazoa, is the existence of a variety of mechanisms with the common quality of being able to recognize the "rightness" of the local situation. Evolution has found ways to ensure the development of sterically complementary molecules or structures which, when mutual recognition occurs, can generate a signal that in essence says "all's well" and inhibits any response evolved to protect the integrity of cell or tissue. It seems likely, in fact, that wherever cells are related to each other as part of the same organism, they must be capable of recognizing the "rightness" of any cell with which they are in persisting or transient contact. This idea could be elaborated considerably in reference to the wandering coelomocytes or hemocytes of the more advanced invertebrates, but for the present all I want to emphasize is that some way must have been invented early in evolution for recognizing self. Implicit in this invention was the potentiality that it could also be used to recognize foreignness by the randomization mechanism, which I shall speak about in the second chapter.

In my opinion there is no convincing evidence of antibody production or of immunological memory in any invertebrate, but there is plenty of evidence that, where it is biologically significant, self can be differentiated from not-self, and "defensive" responses initiated by failure to achieve self-to-self recognition. This, I should point out at once, is a completely different process from the various responses seen in vertebrate immunology as a result of positive recognition by cells of not-self. In a typical invertebrate we have (a) an effective protection against the multiplication of casual microorganisms in the body in which phagocytosis by wandering cells appears to play a part; (b) a variety of not very effective responses to specifically pathogenic microorganisms and metazoan parasites. In general it seems that the invertebrate strategy for species survival is to produce enormous numbers of offspring and accept very large losses from predation, parasitism, and so forth; (c) a limited capacity to recognize self tissue or cells, in the sense that a positive protective or compensatory response occurs when this fails to be achieved. These, then, may have been the basic qualities common to invertebrates from which the vertebrate immune system had to be evolved.

My picture of the way in which the vertebrate system evolved is based to a large extent on Marchalonis's formulation of the facts

(1975) as far as they can be obtained from present day forms. My ideas about the evolutionary process that gave rise to the changes are not dissimilar to his, but I must accept the responsibility for the more picturesque, not to say outrageous, quality of some of my speculations.

I might first state the essential qualities, the parameters of vertebrate immunology, as tabulated by Marchalonis.

1. There are circulating lymphocytes in all vertebrates, and plasma cells in advanced sharks and higher forms.
2. All can produce antibodies.
3. All can reject allografts without the necessity of previous sensitization or immunization. There is, however, quite a sharp difference between the acute rejection seen in mammals and birds and the much slower chronic responses seen in most of the more primitive vertebrate forms.
4. The lymphoid system develops progressively from a minimal requirement of diffuse lymphatic tissue around the gill region—a presumptive anlage of thymus.
5. The ability of antigens bound to antibody to fix complement is seen in all forms above the cyclostomes.

Apart from some equivocal examples of tissue rejection, none of these are found in invertebrates.

Let me begin by stating briefly the general approach to vertebrate immunology that I shall adopt so that I can avoid the necessity of a cumbersome approach from first principles. The justification for adopting one particular set from the variety of alternative interpretations will, I hope, emerge in the course of the chapters that follow. In summary, then:

Most immune reactions are mediated by antibody, i.e., specifically reactive immunoglobulins, in the form either of soluble molecules or as receptors attached to the surface of lymphocytes and other mobile circulating cells. It is assumed that all antibody receptors are synthesized by B cells but that passively acquired immunoglobulins can function as receptors to T lymphocytes, macrophages, and mast cells.

A second distinct system of immune reactivity is concerned not with foreign microorganisms or proteins but with cells of the same species that are differentiated by their major histocompatibility antigens (MHCA's). The corresponding receptors have not yet been chemically characterized and will be referred to as allogeneic receptors (AR's). They are present on and may be limited to T lymphocytes.

The development of the antibody-immunoglobulin system was one of the most fantastically ingenious inventions of evolution. The immunoglobulins seem to be derived from some primitive recognition mechanism based on a rather small protein type referred to now as $\beta 2$ microglobulins. In any modern diagram of a typical antibody, the antibody is shown to be composed of a series of segments or "domains." Each of these has a closely comparable structure of about 110 amino acid residues and a loop formed by a disulphide link between half-cystine residues around positions 30 and 90. The suggestion that each segment represents the result of tandem duplication of a single ancestral gene is compelling. It created great excitement a few years ago when it was found that the major histocompatibility antigen, in both mice and men, was a complex of the antigen proper and a $\beta 2$ microglobulin of essentially similar structure to an immunoglobulin segment. Similar $\beta 2$ microglobulins are widespread in cells, and quite obviously proteins of this sort must resemble closely the gene product of the ancestral gene from which the immunoglobulins evolved.

One can make a few suggestions as to how the immunoglobulin system may have arisen. Even the most primitive stem cell has a reactive cell surface, and it will react more with some chemical structures than with others. No doubt there is at least some potential for specificity in those reactions. The next step in my speculative scheme is a self-recognizing configuration which, though completely symmetrical, has the potentiality of evolving either to (1) a specific individuality marker, a major histocompatibility antigen, or (2) a recognition mechanism, an Ig receptor, or soluble antibody. Like other immunologists, I am puzzled by the nature of the T cell receptor, and at times I see no reason why both sides should not be right—that some undifferentiated T cells not producing Ig can nevertheless "arm themselves" with monomeric IgM (IgM 1) produced by B cells, while others have gone one step further and produce their own IgM 1. For intuitive reasons, however, I should like to think that all T cells received their receptors in passive fashion from B cells in an early stage of stimulation, and I believe that the balance of opinion is swinging rather strongly in that direction. I shall therefore try to follow the implications of the view that the immunoglobulin receptor on T cells is passively derived from B cells. I shall have much more to say about T and B cells in chapter 3 and we can return to some of these points then. The suggestion that mast cells are in a sense postmitotic T cells is one for which I am solely responsible, and it may turn out to be quite wrong. Nevertheless, I have seen changes in thymuses of New Zealand Black (NZB) mice that I could interpret only as direct conversion of thymocytes to mast cells; others have found that thymic cell cultures may sometimes seem to be converted into mast cells, and it is well known that mast cells can be converted into antigen-reactive cells by taking up a few molecules of IgE to serve as receptor.

Considerably less is known about the origin of major histo-compatibility antigens and the corresponding allogeneic receptors. There is a growing feeling that these mutual factors are the only ones concerned with graft-versus-host reactions and mixed lympho-cyte reactions, and in addition that they are important in allogeneic tissue rejection. In these, however, immunoglobulin receptors must also play a part. I am deliberately not going to attempt to elaborate on the nature and evolution of this system of allogeneic receptors. At this stage all I shall say is that it must have evolved in response to some need to be able to distinguish cells of another member of the same species that had intruded within the body. There are at least three possible ways in which this might happen.

The last theme I want to touch on in this preliminary talk is immunological tolerance. As long as an organ is functioning normally, one tends to forget about the controls that must be at work to keep things moving smoothly. It is just one manifestation of this lack of imagination that it took a long time before it was recognized that special mechanisms were necessary to ensure that the immune system did not react against the normal components of the body. I once gained credit for developing the concept that the privileged position of body cells was not just a genetically arranged invulnerability but something that was developed during embryonic and immediately postnatal life. Cell-surface constituents and soluble proteins were not subject to immune attack *because they were there* during the crucial periods of development.

This brings me back to the remark I made earlier about the inability of the embryo to recognize and react to a rather large range of foreign cells and substances. Toward the end of the 19th century, experimental embryologists concerned with *Entwicklungsmechanik* found that it was easy to obtain successful grafts between amphibian embryos of different species, and I have already mentioned similar work with chick embryos. Everything suggests that this quality is common to vertebrate embryos and that the earlier the graft or its equivalent is made, the less evident the response.

The most interesting of all the experiments in this general area are those in which very early embryos at the blastocyst stage, from two completely distinct and immunologically incompatible strains of mice, are brought together under conditions that allow them to fuse into a randomly mixed ball of cells. By some magic beyond our present understanding, the conglomerate adjusts itself so that it produces a physiologically normal mouse while yet assuring that every descendant of the two sets of primary cells manifests its specific qualities just as it would in a normally developed mouse. For complex reasons that I won't elaborate, the movement of pigment cells in such tetraparental or allophenic mouse embryos often results in a distribution of hair color that allows one to talk of zebra mice. What I am interested in, however, is the fact that if two immunologically incompatible strains are used, the two types of cell live together in perfect amity, although it is possible to show, by grafting a piece of skin of an A + B allophene to an A mouse, that the allophenic skin is a finely grained mosaic of A cells and B cells, each retaining its antigenic qualities. Most workers believe that there is no sign of antibody or specific sensitization of cells directed against either of the components. One group, however, finds evidence of cytotoxicity by T cells from such mice against either component in vitro; but in addition an inhibitor, which in vivo completely inhibits any cytotoxic action, is observed. My impression, admittedly a prejudiced one, is that there is a true intrinsic tolerance owing to the absence of specifically cytotoxic cells and that their presence in some systems is either a minor component or possibly an experimental artifact. It is wise, however, to keep that discrepancy firmly in mind as a typical example of the flexibility and complexity of the immune system which almost ensures that when different species, or even different strains of the same species, are used to study the same immunological phenomenon, a proportion of experiments will give quite different answers.

This is even more vividly brought out when the behavior of the fetal and newborn lamb is compared with the standard laboratory rats and mice. Newborn rats fail to reject homografts, and mice are readily rendered tolerant by intravenous injection of allogeneic spleen cells from a neonate of a different strain. The young of these species are born at a relatively immature stage and it is not experimentally practical to test the reactivity of the fetus to antigens. In comparison, the sheep has a long gestation period of 150 days and the lamb is born in a well developed condition. A variety of surgical approaches to fetal experimentation are available, and the results from the two groups, led by Silverstein and Bede Morris respectively, have proved just a little disconcerting to "mouse immunologists" (Silverstein, et al., 1963; Cole and Morris, 1971). Some of them have not yet been satisfactorily integrated into the general pattern of immunological theory.

In the lamb, different antigens differ strikingly in the fetal age at which they are capable of initiating antibody production. Phage X174 is antigenic at the earliest gestational age, 35 days, at which the experiment is practicable. Ferritin becomes immunogenic at 66 days, ovalbumin around 125 days, while an *S. typhosum* vaccine, BCG, and diphtheria toxoid produce no antibody at any time in fetal life or in the first few weeks after birth. Interestingly and somewhat unexpectedly, skin homografts were rejected in normal fashion from the 80th day onward. It must of course be remembered that all these manipulations are very unbiological and the results may have no bearing on general immunology. The only immunological aspects that are likely to have been of evolutionary significance arise from the need for the mother to tolerate paternal antigens in the fetus. It is conceivable that in some species the capacity to handle transplacental infection could also be of evolutionary significance, but human experience suggests that this is not significant for our own species.

Probably all that can be safely concluded is that a correlation exists between the degree of embryonic and fetal development and the nature of the response to antigen. One simple formulation which may be close to the truth is as follows.

1. The earlier the stage of development, the fewer the immunocytes capable of reacting with any foreign pattern.

2. Whenever an antigen can remain present in the body for an indefinite period, reactive immunocytes disappear in fetal or in postnatal life.

3. Active immunocytes are destroyed by relatively smaller doses of cellular or other antigens in fetal life, thus allowing implantation and growth of cells and a constant presence of the foreign antigen.

When I first wrote about tolerance, it seemed a very clear and simple idea. Obviously there must be in early life a phase during which any cells that could attack or produce an antibody against an antigen accessible in the body would be eliminated or at least prevented from proliferating. I suggested that the simplest way of explaining such a process was to assume that an immature immunocyte would overdo its first reaction with antigen and commit suicide; given a chance to avoid the antigen until it was more mature, it would respond by proliferation and antibody production. Under those conditions, everything that was present in the generally accessible fluids and cells of the body would be immediately on hand to eliminate all newly formed cells reactive against them.

Those, however, were unsophisticated days. One of my former colleagues told me not so long ago that he had enumerated 24 different ways by which an animal could be made unresponsive to an antigen that would normally provoke a demonstrable reaction. Many of these certainly had no bearing on the natural tolerance of a healthy animal. But even in natural tolerance, I suspect that more than one mechanism is at work.

Perhaps it is a sign of old age that I am so impressed and daunted by the complexity we meet whenever we try to dig more deeply into biological matters than necessary for our ordinary human purposes. All through the book will run the theme of how the body can successfully carry out the task of differentiating between self and not-self when the difference is often almost infinitesimally small. Immunogeneticists have produced substrains of mice genetically identical except for certain minor genes in a small region of one linkage group. Yet if one injects spleen cells from a mouse of one strain into mice of the second strain, there is a well marked immune response. The presence of one or two antigenic patterns can be recognized from the many thousand potentially antigenic configurations common to both strains. In all lymphoid tissue in which active proliferation is under way, in the thymic cortex or germinal center for example, substantial numbers of cells are dying and rapidly disappear, presumably by enzymic breakdown and solution. In the process hundreds of new potential antigens must become accessible to other lymphocytes, but nothing demonstrable happens. What *could* happen when controls failed to act can be seen in the extraordinary mixture of antibodies against DNA, ribonucleic acid (RNA), and their breakdown products in the autoimmune disease systemic lupus erythematosus (SLE).

That is very nearly all that I want to say in this chapter, but I must complete the moral that I have been working up to. People of today's student generation have been freer of infectious disease during childhood than any other generation, thanks almost wholly to applied immunology. In particular, they are the first generation of adults from whose childhood the threat of polio was lifted. Those various immunizations against smallpox, diphtheria, pertussis, tetanus, polio, and measles have been landmarks of preventive medicine. They rely entirely on immunological processes but required virtually none of our finer modern knowledge of immunology for their success. Their rationale could hardly be simpler. Once the capacity of a mild or completely subclinical infection to protect against subsequent exposure to a highly virulent strain had been established, it was clear that what was needed was simply to imitate a subclinical infection as safely and effectively as possible. And the closer the imitation, the better the promise of immunity— all credit to Albert Sabin for seeing how this could be done against polio. The effect of the Sabin vaccine is simply to produce three harmless but immunizing subclinical infections. May I underline something else—they are imitations of a natural process applied to a genetically normal immune system just moving toward its peak of efficiency at 10 to 12 years of age. Nothing outside the body's standard types of immune response was required. Polio was a pushover, compared with the medical problems in immunology that we are concerned with today. Potentially we could look to immunology for possible control of autoimmune disease, some forms of cancer, and some important aspects of aging. In all of these, however, we are dealing with intrinsic and predominantly genetic processes that have gone wrong, not with a readily understandable impact of a microorganism from the environment. I am not wholly pessimistic, but I shall leave my tentatively hopeful ideas at what may be the bottom of Pandora's box until I have said a good deal about the difficulties in the way. Maybe I shall be proved wrong, but I think I can see, in dim outline, possibilities of our being able to prevent or delay some of the unpleasant aspects of old age if we can understand facts about the immune system, facts that in principle we should be able to discover. If you want a human justification for all the subtle, difficult, and, let us confess, faintly disappointing experimental work on immunology that is being done now, this I think is where you may find it.

CLONAL SELECTION AND ANTIBODY PRODUCTION

I HOPE THAT I MADE it clear in the first chapter that all my discusssion of immunology would be strongly slanted toward a genetic approach. This will hold particularly for anything I say about antibody production and the clonal selection theory. The essence of that theory is that differences between antibodies reflect genetic differences between the cells that produce them. This is now virtually accepted dogma, but it was a full ten years from the time I first published it in 1957 until it was widely accepted. Most immunologists would probably agree that Niels Jerne's final summing up, at the Cold Spring Harbor Symposium on antibodies in 1967, gave it the hallmark of acceptability. Though I only realized it peripherally in 1957, it was essentially a rather straightforward extension of Darwinism to a cellular level.

Perhaps it is not strictly necessary, but I would like to approach the theme of antibody production from a historical point of view. The first man to think hard about the nature of antitoxins, and to a less extent other antibodies, was Paul Ehrlich—the *first* Paul Ehrlich! His suggestion was made at the turn of the century, at a time when genes were unthought of and no one had even reached the stage of wondering how protein could be synthesized. He believed that toxins attached to and exerted their effect on the susceptible cell by combining with "side chains" of a large protoplasmic molecule. If the contact was not lethal, the affected side chain was thrown off and in an overcompensatory reaction many more side chains were produced and liberated as antitoxin. In the light of our present knowledge, the Ehrlich hypothesis is meaningless and cannot be regarded as the prototype of selection theories. The next important step was the work of Landsteiner, on the specificity of serological reactions. This indicated that specific antibodies could be produced against any chemical configuration that could be chemically attached as hapten to a suitable protein carrier. It became impossible to believe that every cell was pre-equipped with side chains to react specifically with every one of the hapten configurations that might be presented to it. The most likely alternative was to assume that the configuration of the antigen itself supplied the "information" from which a complementary pattern could be produced by the cell. The template theories of Breinl and Haurowitz, or of Mudd (proposed between 1930 and 1932), were subsequently refined by Linus Pauling (1940) in the light of the rapidly developing knowledge of protein structure, and it was his version that remained current until the early 1960s. Briefly, Pauling considered that the primary globulin in the form of a long polypeptide chain was brought into contact with an antigen molecule while folding of the chain into its secondary configuration was taking place. This resulted in a "choice" of folding that gave the best fit against the antigen. The chosen configuration was then fixed by the development of S—S or hydrogen bonds and released from the antigen as specific antibody. The antigen molecule could then serve as template for the other end of the polypeptide chain or for another newly produced polypeptide molecule.

Any theory can be only as good as the chemical, genetic, and biological knowledge of the time will allow. Pauling's theory was rightly acclaimed in 1940, but even in 1943, when I first met Pauling in Pasadena, objections were coming into focus. There was already evidence suggesting that the kinetics of antibody production must mean that something was replicating itself, either antibody-producing cells or some subcellular antibody-synthesizing mechanism. It seemed, too, that antibody production could continue long after the antigen had been eliminated, though that is still controversial.

In 1955, Jerne initiated a new approach with his "natural selection theory" of antibody production. In summary, his view was that in any normal serum there was a wide variety of natural antibodies "of unspecified origin" sufficient for at least some to be capable of union with any antigen injected or entering by normal means. Once an antigen–antibody complex formed, it would be ingested by a phagocytic cell, which, by hypothesis, would produce duplicates of the particular natural antibody taken in. The theory had many virtues and played an important part in stimulating me to develop the clonal selection theory, but the mechanism proposed was quite unacceptable. No source was provided for the natural antibodies, and by 1956 it was beginning to be clear that there was no way in which a protein model could be copied directly by a cell. Nevertheless, I should stress that my first paper (1957) was entitled "A modification of Jerne's theory of antibody production using the concept of clonal selection." In order to show that I think that that short paper has stood up well for 18 years I shall cite two paragraphs from it to demonstrate what I meant by clonal selection.

> . . . when an antigen enters the blood or tissue fluids it will attach to the surface of any lymphocytes carrying reactive sites which correspond to one of its antigenic determinants . . . when antigen–natural antibody [i.e., receptor in modern terms] contact takes place on the surface of a lymphocyte the cell is activated to

settle in an appropriate tissue, spleen lymph node or local inflammatory accumulation, and there undergo proliferation to produce a variety of descendants. In this way preferential proliferation will be initiated of all those clones whose reactive sites correspond to the antigenic determinants of the antigens used. The descendants will include plasmacytoid forms capable of active liberation of soluble antibody and lymphocytes that can fulfil the same function as the parental forms [memory cells]. The net result will be a change in the composition of the globulin molecule population to give an excess of molecules capable of reacting with the antigen, in other words the serum will now take on the qualities of specific antibody. The increase in the number of circulating lymphocytes of the clones concerned will also ensure that the response to a subsequent entry of the same antigen will be extensive and rapid.

The theory requires at some stage in early embryonic development a genetic process for which there is no available precedent. In some way we have to picture a randomization of the coding responsible for part of the specification of gamma globulin molecules so that after several cell generations . . . there are specifications in the genomes for virtually every variant that can exist as a gamma globulin molecule. This must then be followed by a phase in which the randomly developed specification is stabilized and transferred as such to descendant cells. At this stage, again following Jerne, any clones of cells which carry reactive sites corresponding to body determinants will be eliminated.

You will discern a slightly old fashioned flavor about this excerpt, but I think you can also see that it is still a valid description of the broad theory of antibody diversity and antibody production, now so generally accepted that it has become dogma of the Establishment. However, it took ten years, as I said earlier, before a majority accepted it. Looking back, I find it very interesting that most of the experiments designed to prove that the clonal selection hypothesis was false appeared to do so, but that with each successive year some new finding emerged that fitted perfectly into the pattern of clonal selection. I think the moral is that you should read Karl Popper's ideas* about how hypotheses must be tested; but remember the complexity of things biological, and do not be too willing to

*See Bryan Magee, *Karl Popper*, Viking, New York, 1973, for a convenient short account of Popper's philosophy.

accept the first "disproof" of your hypothesis as necessarily the end of the story.

That is enough about the historical side, which can really interest only my contemporaries, and, of course, me! Let me now try to tell you the approximate position today, beginning with the structure of the antibody molecule. All the immunoglobulins are made up of a set of similar units equivalent to a $\beta 2$ microglobulin of about 110 amino acid residues, and it is probable that they are all coded for by mutant descendants of a single primitive gene. These subunits of immunoglobulin are now generally referred to as domains. Two domains are found in all light chains, four in IgG γ-heavy chain, and five in IgM μ-heavy chain. As you know from the standard diagram of an antibody, the segment at the N terminal end of both light and heavy chains is said to be a variable V segment, whereas the others are constant C. One needs to recognize that V and C have a rather special meaning in this context. They refer to the degree of similarity of the sequence of amino acid residues in corresponding domains of a series of ten or more purified antibodies. (In practice these purified antibodies are obtained from myeloma proteins, which I shall discuss shortly, but it is quite legitimate to think of them simply as a purified sample of a single type of antibody molecule.) If we look at the sequences of those ten antibodies and start from the N terminal end, the first segment will show wide variations from one antibody to another. At position 27, for instance, our ten examples might have any one of five different amino acid residues in that position.

There is another aspect of the V domains, which is easily recognized in any extensive set of amino acid sequences and which must have some significance for the process by which diversity is achieved. This is the existence of hypervariable regions. In the human kappa light chain are three regions, each extending over six to eleven positions, where the variability is much more striking than elsewhere. In the heavy-chain V segment there are four such hypervariable regions. The V regions are followed by appropriate numbers of 105- to 110-unit C domains which are almost identical from one immunoglobulin to any other of the same type (M, G,

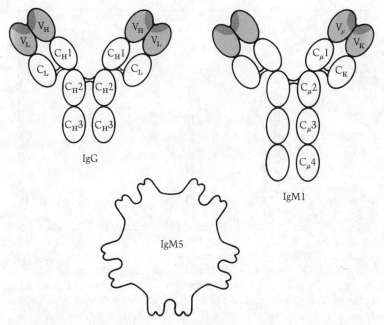

FIGURE 2–1. *The construction of immunoglobulin G and monomeric immunoglobulin M from V and C domains, arranged in light and heavy chains united by disulphide bonds. The way in which five IgM1 units are combined to form standard pentameric IgM is also indicated.*

A, etc.). There are, however, a very small number of positions at which a choice between one of two alternatives exists. As I indicated in the first chapter, these domains are probably the end result of a long process of evolutionary development beginning with what is known as tandem duplication of the original gene for $\beta 2$ microglobulin.

For the present we need think about only the commonest and most simply constructed class of antibody, the G, or γ, immunoglobulin group. As a very rough estimate Jerne (1971) has suggested that in the course of any human life about a million differentiable sorts of antibody are probably produced and that the whole potential of the species might be 100 to 1000 times that number. Under the circumstances it was natural to think that it

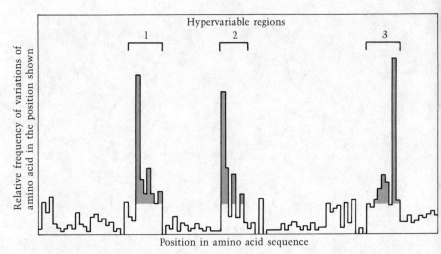

FIGURE 2–2.   *The hypervariable regions in the V domain of human kappa light chain. The degree of variability in each of the 107 positions is shown by the height of the bar; where no bar is present, all amino acid residues at that position are the same in the 20 to 30 light chains tested. Shaded bars indicate the three hypervariable regions. [Modified from Wu and Kabat, 1970.]*

was the diversity of pattern in the variable chains that was responsible for specificity. This appears to be accurate. If you have 20 different amino acid residues capable of occupying each of 110 positions in a polypeptide chain, there could be, theoretically, 20^{110} different patterns, a quite unimaginable number. And no matter in how many ways you restrict the possibilities, a number of potentialities far beyond the million or two we need must always remain. We must remember also that the combining site of an antibody molecule is composed of *two* juxtaposed variable domains, each with the same high potentiality of diversity. Recently X-ray diffraction methods have yielded direct evidence that a hapten molecule bound to a corresponding pure antibody lies in a shallow groove or crevice between the L and H variable chains. The hypervariable regions seem to form the surface elements of the groove that are most directly related to the antigenic determinant.

May I make a slight interpolation here. It should perhaps amaze us more than it does, that, by taking a mere 20 amino acids and stringing them together in a linear sequence, nature has produced something that can become a high-affinity specific absorbent for *any* type of organic, and some inorganic, steric configurations. Of all the possible amino acids, how and why were these 20 chosen? The superficial answer is, of course, that they were the ones whose linear polymers were best suited for the task of "recognizing" any other chemical configuration when they were in their standard three-dimensional form, so making possible the development of enzymes, antibodies, hormones, and receptors. The process by which this was achieved in the first phase of evolution is, of course, quite unknown, but its development may well have occupied most of the first billion years after the earth became potentially suitable for life.

Irrespective of how and when proteins evolved, we are compelled to locate antibody specificity on the variable domains and to assume that the variability in amino acid sequence from one antibody to the next is the basis of that specificity. This in turn relegates to the genome the problem of how diversity of antibody pattern arises. There is no possibility that any "instruction" by an intruding foreign antigen can produce structural changes involving amino acid replacements. The diversity must be the result of genetic processes, some having taken place in the course of evolution and transmitted in the germ line, others having been carried out in the somatic cells ancestral to lymphocytes in the course of development and in adult life. At the present time there are at least four theories on the nature of those genetic processes.

1. The first is that *all* the V gene patterns are stored in the genome, having arisen by duplication and independent mutation in the whole course of vertebrate evolution (Hood and Prahl, 1971). All the other theories assume that, although all the general features of immunoglobulins are genetically determined, most of the variation from one V domain to another arises by processes in the somatic genome during the embryonic and fetal differentiation of the lymphocytes of the immune system, but the possibilities envisaged are themselves quite diverse.

2. The suggestion by Wu and Kabat (1970) is that the hyper-variable regions represent insertions of segments of oligonucleotides from a store somewhere else in the genome. This seems to have no reasonable analogies with any other genetic process, and though it was the first serious attempt to explain the presence of the hypervariable regions, it has few supporters at the present time.

3. Gally and Edelman (1970) looked for interactions among a relatively small store of germ-line genes coding for alternative domains. This could take the form of intrachromosomal recombination and crossing over and could in principle allow an almost unlimited number of new patterns to be generated. The approach is based on the occurrence of similar processes in bacterial genetics, but there is no direct evidence to support the hypothesis. Milstein and Munro (1973) believe that it is inadmissible.

4. Somatic mutation was suggested in my first papers on clonal selection and has been supported by Milstein and Munro (1973). Most of those interested in such theories have assumed that a very high rate of somatic mutation and/or some specific mechanism must be postulated. This is probably correct, but it is worth noting that the apparent high rate of mutation could wholly or in part reflect the fact that in this system, and only this system, *any* point mutation may have a specific and potentially demonstrable effect. Most single nucleotide replacements in somatic cells give rise to no observable result, and in consequence are not considered in any calculations of somatic mutation rates.

However, as will be evident in a subsequent chapter, I believe that we have an obligation to look beyond a simple statement that a given phenomenon is due to somatic mutation and look for at least some molecular interpretation of its occurrence. A notable suggestion in this field has been offered by David Baltimore (1974). In his view the presence of the enzyme terminal deoxyribonucleotidyl transferase (TDT), a type of DNA polymerase, in the thymus and, in smaller amounts, in bone marrow but in no other normal tissue may indicate that it acts as a mutagen to produce antibody diversity. If we assume the presence of an endonuclease coded to recognize certain points on the variable gene and making a "nick" to initiate a limited removal by an exonuclease of 2 to 10 nucleotides, a space is available to be filled by the TDT enzyme. This acts by inserting a nucleotide at random unlike any normal DNA polymerase, which of course is guided by the opposite strand as template. Such a mechanism provides an impressive explanation of the well marked phenomenon in the variable chains of one position at the end of a hypervariable region with many more alternative amino acid residues than any of the others. This could mark the point recognized by the initiating endonuclease where the variable deletion begins to be eventually refilled at random by TDT enzyme. In a sense this is somatic mutation at a "hot spot." A thought that may be worth bearing in mind when I come to the discussion of error-prone DNA polymerases in chapter 5 is that TDT may be derived from an exceptionally error-prone DNA polymerase which found a useful niche for this special purpose in the immunocyte line.

As will be evident, my own position is to favor the Milstein-Baltimore approach and look to somatic mutation of a rather special type to provide the numbers of additional patterns that are required beyond what can be selected from the genetic store. But it is a preference that one good new review of the problem could swing into a different direction.

Monoclonal Gammopathies

In 1847, an English physician, Henry Bence-Jones, sent a specimen of urine to a chemical pathologist and received a report that it contained an unusual type of protein in large amount. The patient had multiple bone tumors, and by putting two and two together Bence-Jones introduced a useful diagnostic method for multiple myelomatosis, and immortalized his name. It took more than a hundred years, however, before it was known that here was the most interesting of all "natural" proteins, a soluble protein, often present with only minimal amounts of other proteins and composed of a population of *identical* molecules. In due course it was found that similar but usually larger molecules were present in the blood and that sometimes there was no evidence of the bone tumors (multiple myelomas). Jan Waldenström, around 1960, spoke of the whole group of conditions as monoclonal gammopathies, making the obvious deduction, from the uniformity of the abnormal protein present, that it was derived wholly from cells springing from a single progenitor.

This proposal was quite rapidly accepted, and I think that most pathologists and immunologists now believe such conditions arise from the mutation (or some equivalent change) in a single antibody-producing cell, causing it to proliferate more actively and more persistently than normal. Sometimes the proliferative drive over-steps the bounds and becomes a malignant condition, but, irrespective of whether the change is malignant or reasonably benign, each cell of the clone produces antibody globulin of identical structure. There are many variants in this group of diseases, and present-day opinion is tending to recognize a whole range of monoclonal proliferations of B cell derivatives, from malignant reticulum cell sarcomas, from which immunoglobulins can be demonstrated, to chronic lymphocytic leukemia, Waldenström's macroglobulinemia, and classical multiple myelomatosis.

I am certain that if these monoclonal antibodies and monoclonal populations of the cells producing them had not existed, or if they had been much rarer than they are, the clonal selection theory would probably still be a matter of controversy. As it happened, with every increase in the number studied and with each refinement of chemical and immunological technique, it became increasingly clear that we had available a unique way to test and confirm the theory. Several hundred, possibly a thousand, monoclonal immu-noglobulins, each from a different patient, have now been studied with varying degrees of sophistication. Perhaps the easiest way to sum up the results is to say that if one mixed a milligram of each of those thousand pure proteins and compared it with a gram of mixed immunoglobulins from pooled normal serum no significant differ-ences would be found. IgG, IgM, IgA, and IgD myeloma proteins are found, in that order of diminishing frequency, just as they are in normal serum. There are even two—or maybe more now—IgE myeloma proteins. It seems that the process by which B cell is, as it were, touched on the shoulder and told to multiply without limit is wholly at random. It can happen to anyone.

For a time it seemed strange that none of the myeloma proteins was an antibody, but it is now clear that only a little patience and the use of many antigens was necessary to find them. Many are now known. I think one of my happiest moments was at the Cold Spring Harbor Symposium in 1967. In my opening talk, written of course some months previously, I had stated that I would "predict that with appropriate study many myeloma proteins would be shown to be antibodies of low avidity for definable antigenic determinants." The first of these, against dinitrophenyl (DNP), was described by Eisen et al. (1967) at that very meeting, and they have become commonplace since.

More recently, what most people would consider more normal monoclonal antibodies have been obtained in both rabbits and mice. A proportion of rabbits immunized with streptococcal or pneumococcal antigens give sera containing exceptional amounts of monoclonal antibody. Further study showed that, particularly in neonatal rabbits, antibody against DNP was monoclonal in 50 percent of the cases. The simplest and most likely explanation is probably the rarity of antigen-reactive cells with that particular specificity in the circulating population of lymphocytes.

A more sophisticated method of obtaining and manipulating a single clone of antibody-producing cells was worked out by Askonas et al. in 1970. This depended on transferring limited numbers of spleen cells from normal mice to heavily irradiated syngeneic recipients along with an antigen made by combining the synthetic hapten DNP with a standard natural protein, bovine gamma-globulin. In a proportion of the mice producing antibody against DNP, isoelectric focusing techniques showed monoclonal antibody and transfer of spleen cells from such mice to another irradiated recipient with antigen gave a similar response. This passage could be continued for seven passes and then regularly failed.

How Many Antibody Types Are There?

I suspect that any limit to the number of different antibody molecules that an individual animal can produce is meaninglessly high and that the total repertoire of the species is a good many times higher than that. I have previously mentioned the enormous figures that would be calculated from all the potentialities of 20 different amino acids on two randomly interacting chains of 100 + positions each. There are two commonly quoted experimental results. Kreth and Williamson (1973) produced monoclonal sera to DNP in large numbers of mice; these were characterized physically by isoelectric focusing. Of 337 antibodies, 327 were found only once, five occurred in apparent identity in two mice each. The result of course depended on how sensitive this technique was in detecting differences, but the authors' calculations were that the antibodies seemed to be drawn from a potential pool of 3000 to 30,000 antibodies against the one synthetic hapten. The second experiment is to produce a specific antibody against a human myeloma protein (antibody): in most cases this will not detect that antigenic determinant in any normal human serum.

There is no doubt about the unlimited number of molecular configurations that can be present in the variable segments of antibodies. And, as can be gathered from Kreth and Williamson's experiment, for any given antigenic determinant there are many thousands of different antibodies that can react with it. Conversely, if one tests a single myeloma protein, i.e., a uniform population of antibody molecules that reacts with DNP, against a series of more or less closely related haptens, many will react, each with a characteristic affinity. According to Eisen, one occasionally finds an apparently quite unrelated chemical configuration that will react. I hope this will let you see what an extremely difficult concept immunological specificity is to define—or to understand. A diagram that I showed at the antibody meeting at Cold Spring Harbor may be helpful (Figure 2-3). It gives the frequency distribution of Ig molecules in an antiserum according to the affinity of their union with the antigenic determinant responsible. Only those in the right-hand end of the curve will be judged as antibody, but the cutoff point toward the left will depend on the qualities of the method used to detect the immune response. It is a very useful diagram to have in front of you when you are thinking about cross-reactions.

In the next chapter I shall be speaking of B and T cells, but something should be said here about the cells which produce antibody. They all belong to the group we call B cells but show two distinct

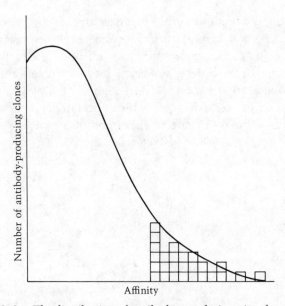

FIGURE 2–3.   *The distribution of antibody populations (or clones of cells producing them) in the blood of an immunized individual, according to their affinity for a single antigenic determinant. In such a notional diagram only those antibody types corresponding to the squares will be demonstrable experimentally.*

types of morphology with some intermediates. B cells proper are lymphocytes of various degrees of activity which are capable both of multiplication and of producing their specific antibody in relatively small amount. Plasma cells are derivatives of B cells that have become specialized factories for the production of antibody. As structural evidence of this they are densely packed with "rough endoplasmic reticulum," the morphological sign of active protein synthesis by a cell. Plasma cells tend to settle down in lymphoid tissue, particularly in the medullary cord region of lymph nodes. In general they are postmitotic cells that have lost the ability to multiply but go on producing antibody, sometimes for several weeks.

In this chapter I have been talking essentially about antibody. In many ways it is the best understood segment of immunology and I shall be surprised if any serious changes will need to be made in our present conceptions of the chemistry and genetics of antibody and of the physiology of its production. As in every area, the difficulties that arise relate to the *control* of its production and functioning. In those fields we have a lot to learn and much that may be too subtly in accord with the whole quality of the living organism for us ever to be able to understand in depth. In the next chapter I shall make a start on that impossible task.

T AND B CELLS

IN THE CURRENT immunological journals one will find about half the papers concerned with some aspect of T and B cell function. Perhaps it is being overdone. Some immunologists begin to wonder whether the differentiation into those two groups is as sharp as we tend to think it, and before I end this chapter I shall probably voice a few heresies. However, for the present it is an extremely useful convention and in one form or another will persist. I am probably unduly interested in the topic on the grounds that much of the basic work that led to the definition of the two cell types took place in Australia. I think you will find that the first paper indicating the difference resulted from work done in my laboratory by Warner and Szenberg (1961), and that the use of T and B grew out of the paper Warner gave in 1962 at the Minneapolis meeting on the immunobiology of the thymus. B stood for bursa of Fabricius, and T for thymus. Removal of bursal function by administration of testosterone to the embryo resulted in failure of the chicken to produce antibody when tested two or three months after hatching but left it able to reject skin homografts and to produce graft-versus-host reactions on the chorioallantois. I should mention here an almost unnoticed feature of Warner and his coworkers' results, which I hope you will bear in mind because it is highly relevant to the discussion later in this chapter. Bursectomized chickens with intact thymuses failed to produce tuberculin sensitization or give a typical vaccinia response—two classical examples of what we nowadays call T cell responses. We and the rest of the world have tended to forget this little discrepancy and have been content to let the two qualities, B for antibody production, T for the production of graft-versus-host reactions, be the main points for differentiating T cell function from B cell function.

People had been thinking about the function of the thymus for years, and there were thoughts in many minds that it should have an immunological function. But all the standard experiments of removing the thymus surgically from various species of animal gave no definite results until J. F. A. P. Miller (1961), an Australian who was working in England at the time, discovered that removing the thymus from mice within 24 hours of birth left them immunologically crippled, particularly in their inability to reject allografts of skin. Since then, the neonatally thymectomized mouse has been a standard experimental object. The first evidence of the need for cooperation between T and B cells, if antibody was to be produced normally, came from Claman et al. (1966), but Mitchell and Miller (1968) were close on his heels in work done in the Walter and Eliza Hall Institute.

That is enough history. We can now examine the functional aspects that differentiate T from B cells. I shall say little more about B cells, which were the central theme of the preceding chapter on clonal section. A serious difficulty we face in dealing with T cells is that they are never available as monoclonal populations. Whatever we study is a mixture. Whether it is a suspension of cells from spleen or thymus, thoracic duct fluid or lymphocytes from the circulating blood, it will contain T cells directed against a range of different antigens in much the same way as B cells are. And there will certainly be other functional differences, such as that between cooperator cells and suppressor cells. It is even very hard to give a wholly satisfactory definition of a T cell. To say it must have descended from a cell that differentiated in the thymus does not allow any direct criterion to be applied to an actual cell population elsewhere than in the thymus itself, and in the sheep there is no real evidence that the cells subserving similar functions in that animal are all of thymic origin.

In mid-1974 a controversy on the nature of the immune receptors on T cells arose that remains unresolved. Benacerraf and a majority of American immunologists are of the opinion that T cells have a receptor that is neither an immunoglobulin nor an Ig derivative. Marchalonis, Greaves, and others claim that immunoglobulin is on the surface, that it is a monomeric form of IgM, and that it can be shown to be synthesized by the T cell which carries it. Both sides accept the presence of other types of receptor.

Before giving my own particular version, I should say what I have often said in criticism of others—that until we know how to recognize, prepare, and manipulate monoclonal populations of T cells, and until we have decided whether an immunoglobulin receptor is indeed present, any suggested interpretation is wholly tentative. However, I think that there is some virtue in perpetually trying to choose and support the best current interpretation, simply because without hypotheses it is very difficult to devise experiments that are going to help clarify the position.

The first general statement I would make is that if specific antibody production is the main function of B cells, the role of T cells is to synthesize and liberate pharmacologically active substances, "lymphokines," in such a way that cell reactions relevant to the immune system are influenced. T cells are executive or effector cells insofar as they can kill cells carrying foreign antigens, but they can function equally well as regulator cells to cooperate with or suppress antibody-producing cells, or to suppress, if necessary, cytotoxic T cells. Another regulatory function for T cells is to provide a constant supply of undifferentiated T cells that can be recruited to whatever function is immediately required. This recruitment function has been mentioned occasionally, but I don't think that others have attached as much importance to it as I do.

Let me say something about the recognized activities of T cells, first reminding you of my earlier remark, that almost every generalization one can make about immunological phenomena is soft edged: if it is 90 percent true, it has the status that in physics or chemistry is reserved for generalizations that can predict quantitative consequences accurate to 1 in 1000 or better. I find the easiest way to see what the T cell can do is to look at three sample situations—one taken from human pathology and two from experiments with animals.

First, in the condition called congenital sex-linked agammaglobulinemia—it affects only boys—the ability to produce antibody to the usual immunizing agents is lacking, and the level of immunoglobulin in the blood plasma is very low, although never completely absent. Also small amounts of IgE are present, and allergy to ragweed has been reported. Lymph nodes show no plasma cell response to a vaccine injection.

Symptoms in such children may be due to the lack of immunoglobulin and antibody. These include the repeated bacterial infections, especially pneumonia, that, before the introduction of antibiotics, were always fatal. The T cells, which appear to be normal, must be responsible for the long list of immune functions that show no significant deficiency or abnormality. Measles and other common viral diseases, including vaccination against smallpox, run a normal course and are followed by the typical long-lasting immunity to the disease. Allografts of skin are rejected, though somewhat more slowly than normal, and sensitization to standard skin-sensitizing agents, such as DNFB, is readily achieved.

There is no way in which a condition similar to agammaglobulinemia, essentially due to absence of functioning B cells, can be produced in a mammalian model. Early inhibition by testosterone or surgical removal of the avian bursa results in failure to produce antibody, but nothing equivalent to the bursa is present in a mammal. It is, however, practical to remove the thymus at an early age and produce an experimental model of T-cell deficiency. Surgical removal of the thymus from mice less than 24 hours after birth effectively removes from consideration all the cells that would have developed to T cells therein.

The third example is the sheep. The lamb is of course born in a vastly more developed state than the mouse, but in the larger animal surgical interference in utero is quite practicable, and Morris and his colleagues in the Australian National University have been able to remove the thymus completely at about one third of the way through the period of gestation (Cole and Morris, 1971). As Morris likes to point out, the fetus, after operation, is returned to a warm, moist container where it has the best conceivable postoperative care in a sterile environment. He contrasts it with the neonatal mouse, anesthetized by cold and introduced unprepared to the onslaught of all the bacteria of the environment. The lamb is born normally and thrives, it rejects skin grafts normally, and has no difficulty in making antibody responses to all antigens in parallel with those from normal lambs. None of the responses that are regarded from studies on man and mouse as requiring the activities of T cells are absent. Three effects, however, are noted by Morris: *first*, the level of circulating lymphocytes and the weight of lymphoid tissue at birth is only one-third to one-quarter the normal value, and only slowly rises, being still below normal at one year; *second*, delayed hypersensitivity reactions in the skin are positive, but inflammation and cellular infiltration are much lower than in normal lambs; *third*, injection of lymphocytes from an unrelated sheep into the skin of a fetally thymectomized lamb gives a visibly positive lymphocyte transfer reaction, but again it is far less active than the violent reaction seen in a normal recipient.

The only interpretation of the sheep findings that makes sense to me is that T cells can arise in other primary lymph tissue, in addition to the thymus, elsewhere in the body. A likely site could be in the highly developed lymphoid tissue of the gut, which is conspicuous in late fetal life. Enough cells are produced elsewhere than in the thymus to allow adequate T cell functions. Nevertheless, the neonatal thymus in the sheep is a large and very active organ that must be pouring large numbers of lymphocytes into the circulation. Although it is clear that they are not vitally necessary, they are presumably useful for emergencies which can be regarded as more or less adequately represented by the model systems, delayed hypersensitivity and lymphocyte transfer reaction, mentioned above. The suggestion arises immediately that the great bulk of lymphocytes released from the sheep thymus, and, by extension, from the thymus of any young animal, are neutral T cells that can be recruited to some or any of the functions within T cell capability. This recruitment function should be kept in mind, because it has an important function in the scheme that seems best to draw the phenomena into logical form, and with which I shall finish this chapter.

The Problem of the Ig Receptor on the T Cell

Until the problem of the Ig receptor on the T cell is satisfactorily solved, we shall get nowhere in understanding T cell behavior; let us therefore examine the difficulties. The simplest way to tell whether a single lymphocyte is B or T is to test it with fluorescent antibody against immunoglobulin. If it is a human lymphocyte, we use a rabbit antiserum against human immunoglobulin. B cells fluoresce readily, whereas T cells with standard technique show no fluorescence. In addition, for some rather obscure reason, human T cells are sticky for sheep red blood cells, which form rosettes around them, whereas B cells are not. The reaction on the B cell surface is ascribed to Ig receptors, which act as the means by which antigen can stimulate the cell to respond. Suitable experiment shows it to be the same type as that secreted by the cell, and the question arises whether it is not merely Ig in the process of being secreted, and not necessarily related to receptors at all. At least some immunologists would agree that it is still rather an article of faith than an established fact that the B cell immune receptor is simply a homologous antibody linked in some way to a surface unit capable of generating a signal to initiate cellular response. This doubt about B cell receptors will of course increase the difficulty of solving the T cell problem.

There is no question that small amounts of immunoglobulin can be obtained from cell populations containing 90 percent or more of T cells by methods designed to remove it from the cell surface. I accept the findings of Marchalonis and Cone (1973) and others that much of this immunoglobulin is an 8S monomeric form of IgM known to be present intracellularly in relatively large amount as the penultimate stage in the biosynthesis of standard pentameric IgM. The evidence of synthesis of immunoglobulin by at least some of the cells in the experimental population is acceptable, but this population is never a homogeneous one. One must also remember the finding of Nossal and Pike (1975) that in the bone marrow there are cells with no evidence of immunoglobulin on their surfaces which subsequently become positive. If we could work with a monoclonal population of T cells, the results would be much more readily interpreted, and work is in progress in at least two laboratories on monoclonal tumors of T cells. Haustein et al. (1974) found that two such tumors of mice gave evidence of rather large amounts of immunoglobulin, along with adequate evidence that this can be synthesized by the cell itself. It would seem to be ungracious not to accept this as final, but unfortunately when one is dealing with two sorts of somatic cells, A and B, from a single stem cell line, it is dangerous to assume that when A becomes malignant it will retain all the characters that differentiate normal A from normal B. It is axiomatic that A, B, and their common stem cell contain all the genetic information concerned with differential characters between A and B, and it is well known that neoplastic cells will not infrequently synthesize proteins and antigens that their normal cells of origin did not produce. It seems that argument on T cell receptors cannot be based on chemical studies but on the systematic analysis of specific reactivity with antigens.

The great majority of antigens require the cooperation of B and T lymphocytes and macrophages for optimal antibody production, and virtually all the theorizing and experimentation in this field have been based on the assumption that T and B cells both need to be specifically reactive with the antigen concerned. The only simple explanation is that the effective receptor on both cell types is the same, and, by implication, of immunoglobulin nature. There is no doubt about the capacity of B cells to synthesize immunoglobulin, but, as we have seen, there is serious doubt as to the capacity of T cells. Logically, Ig receptors on T cells could be of two distinct origins: (1) a receptor could be synthesized by the cell itself; (2) it could be passively acquired from an activated B cell.

In comparing the alternatives, much depends on how decisively the evidence supports the opinion that, in cooperation, both cells specifically react with the same determinant of the antigen. Admittedly, when the antigen is an artificial combination of a hapten and a carrier protein or synthetic peptide, the T cell is mainly or solely reactive with determinants on the carrier portion, but this cannot hold for the natural proteins and other antigens that the immune system was presumably evolved to deal with. If we accept the view that for optimal response T and B cells must have receptors of the same specificity, a difficult problem arises in the first stages of an immune response to an antigen not previously experienced. There will be very few of the appropriate cells in the circulating populations, and it will be extremely unlikely that chance will bring into threefold contact, somewhere in the lymphoid tissues, a macrophage carrying the antigen or involved in some other fashion, a B cell and a T cell, both with the same appropriate receptor; that is, if the immune patterns arose independently of one another by a random process.

Simple a priori reasoning suggests that the problem would be easier for evolution to solve if both B and T cells could receive their Ig receptors from a common source. The only reasonable possibility that I can conceive is that if a B cell with the correct type of receptor is stimulated to synthesize monomeric IgM in the cytoplasm and to liberate small amounts into the immediate vicinity, this could in theory become attached to any uncommitted T cells in the area. Associated with each initially stimulated B cell, therefore, one would expect to find a small group of T cells "armed" passively with receptors exactly equivalent to those on the B cells. These would be available to provide the extra stimulus needed for the B cells to move on to a more active IgM liberation followed by the switch to IgG, for which T cooperation appears to be vital. This sort of reasoning provides one justification for thinking of T cells not as active synthesizers of immunoglobulin but as passive recipients of the immunoglobulin produced by adjacent B cells.

So far I have not mentioned what happens in the rat, which, after the mouse, is the most widely used experimental animal in immunological research. Less than a year ago, a series of papers from Gowans' laboratory in Oxford appeared dealing with T cells in the rat, which showed, I think, definitively that in the rat T cells synthesized no immunoglobulin. The work of Hunt and Williams (1974) depends essentially on the discovery of a light chain allotype in the rat. In some animals there are two or more alternative forms of functionally similar immunoglobulin which are differentiated by tests with antibody made against the immunoglobulin in another animal of the same species; these different forms are known as allotypes. This allows the experimenters to use rat strains whose major histocompatibility types and allotypes were as shown:

Strain	HCA	Allotype
PVG	B5	Ig Ib
DA	B4	Ig Ia
AO	B2	Ig Ib

In the experiments, purified antibodies against Ig Ia that could detect that allotype exclusively were prepared and tested with appropriate controls. Lymphocytes from thoracic duct lymph of F1 (PVG × DA) were studied. As in the parent strains, these cells were divisible into two categories, one binding 100 to 2000 molecules of antibody per cell (presumptive T cells) and the other 10^4 to 10^5 molecules (B cells). In the F1 lymphocytes the heavily binding cells showed allelic exclusion, i.e., they showed about half that bound Ig Ia; the rest (35 to 40 percent) failed to do so, but would presumably have been recognized by an anti-Ig Ib antibody if it had been available. On the other hand there was no sign of this exclusion with the lightly labeled T cells. An equivalent finding that pointed to the absence of synthesis of immunoglobulin was obtained by injecting thoracic duct lymphocytes of one allotype into irradiated recipients of the opposite allotype. Under these circumstances the recovered B cells still showed their proper (donor) allotype, but the lightly binding T cells had now exchanged immunoglobulin of donor allotype for that of the host. It was clear that the T cells carried small amounts of reversibly bound immunoglobulin and did not synthesize it. Hunt and Williams have thus shown that some 90 percent of T cells do not synthesize immunoglobulin, and there is some indirect evidence that this might hold for all.

For practical purposes, or for selecting the most consistent finding on which to base generalizations about immunity or to construct the most acceptable outline for teaching immunology, I shall have to adopt the rule that the T cell does not synthesize the immunoglobulin on its surface. However, what the function of that passively obtained IgM may be remains to be discussed. My own ideas on this subject have been largely influenced by the possibility that the interaction of mast cells and basophils with IgE, the immunoglobulin primarily concerned with allergic reactions in man and analogous responses in other mammals, could provide a model for the relationship of T cells to IgM.

Ten years ago I made a queer discovery (Burnet, 1965) that no one has ever confirmed but that I have continued to feel was important. At the time I was interested in lesions of the thymuses of New Zealand Black (NZB) mice and was examining most of the mice killed in the course of various experiments from this point of view. All the thymuses had a few mast cells, often in small elongate clumps of 6 or 10 cells, there being more cells in males than in females and very few in young animals of either sex not yet showing a positive Coombs test. But in addition there were two thymuses with large areas in which thymocytes seemed to have been converted en masse to mast cells, and two more in which less extensive but obviously similar changes were taking place. After staining sections in various ways, I came to the conclusion that there had been a change in situ of thymocytes to mast cells and that the process spread peripherally from a central area of initiation by the diffusion of something from a cell undergoing mast cell transformation to adjacent normal appearing cells. As is usual with mast cells, the nuclei in hematoxylin-eosin sections showed no trace of mitosis. This seems to exclude any possibility of a semimalignant infiltration and proliferation by mast cells from somewhere else.

If my interpretation is correct, one is virtually compelled to call mast cells—or at least the mast cells that developed in those thymuses—T cells. Since 1974 I have been looking seriously for evidence to support the hypothesis that mast cells are postmitotic T cells with something of the same relationship to the standard T cells that plasma cells have to B lymphocytes.

In the first place, mitosis or evidence of DNA synthesis is very rarely seen in mast cells, except in mastocytomas, a fact indicating their proliferation in some other morphological guise. The only well known situation in which one finds heavy accumulations of mast cells is in the intestinal wall of rats with an infestation by the nematode *Nippostrongylus* at a time just preceding the phenomenon of immunological "self-cure." Miller and Jarrett (1971) state that the cells arrive at this site in the form of lymphoblast-like cells.

Mast cells have a tendency to be found where immunological activities of T cells are to be expected, e.g., adjacent to skin cancers in mice or in the thymuses of NZB mice. Examining lymph nodes some months after a local immune response, Miller and Cole (1968) found mast cells labeled with tritiated thymidine given at the time of the antigen injection. Recently there has been considerable interest in the type of skin hypersensitivity to certain antigens in guinea pigs that is referred to as a Jones-Mote reaction. Sections of such reactions show many infiltrating cells, of which 25 percent or more are mast cells or basophils.

The main objection to the suggestion that mast cells are mature T lymphocytes seems to be that basophil leucocytes, which functionally behave like mast cells, are generally regarded as granulocytes. I do not think that this is fatal to the hypothesis; it is not impossible that more than one type of cell may adopt a common structural feature.

Immunologically, the most important quality of mast cell (and basophil leucocyte) is its ability to take up IgE antibody in specific fashion, presumably by the Fc moiety, to form an Ig receptor, which on contact with the corresponding allergen generates a signal for rapid degranulation and discharge of histamine and/or serotonin. Here then is an unequivocal instance in which a well defined cell type attaches to its surface one particular type of antibody (IgE), and, apart from a much less active binding of one of the IgG variants in rodents (different ones in rats and mice), it is specific for IgE antibodies alone. Once attached, the IgE has become a sensitive receptor, stimulation of which results in the liberation of active pharmacological agents into the immediate environment.

One is driven to ask whether this could perhaps be a model of what happens with T cells generally. It does not seem out of character, with the way evolution works, for newly differentiated T cells to have, for a limited period, the capacity to attach freshly liberated monomeric IgM in such a fashion that it becomes an effective receptor. In this way we could have a population of T cells which (a) would have the surface immunoglobulin found by Marchalonis, and (b) could in principle cooperate with B cells in the fashion described by Mitchell and Miller (1968). Determination of the correctness of that suggestion must wait on the development of an effective experimental approach. The crucial requirement is still to have available a monoclonal population of nonmalignant T cells.

There are, however, phenomena involving specific responses of T cells in which Ig receptors seem to play no part. My own interest in the matter arose, as I have already indicated, from work on the response of the chick embryo membrane to adult chicken leucocytes. When one can work with eggs and adult fowls of a single pure-line strain, it can be shown that leucocytes, usually in the form of heparinized blood from a grown chicken, deposited on the chorioallantoic membrane of embryos of the same strain, provoke no reaction whatever. A sharp response is seen, however, if embryos of another pure-line or random outbred embryos are used and $\frac{1}{20}$ milliliter is deposited on the membrane. In two days' time usually

20 to 200 opaque foci will be scattered over each membrane. It is clear that this is a recognition of foreignness, and therefore almost by definition an immunological response. But it has some disconcerting qualities that Simonsen (1962) has emphasized.

The reaction is regarded as primarily a graft-versus-host reaction. A lymphocyte of the adult donor is capable of recognizing a major histocompatibility antigen different from its own. It reacts by the liberation of irritant lymphokines and by proliferating. Embryonic cells are attracted to the irritated area and a local cellular accumulation, easily visible to the naked eye, results. The reaction soon subsides, and by five or six days the lesions are becoming fibrous nodules on the way to necrosis. The difficulty of interpreting the reaction in terms of a simple clonal selection theory of immunity was that there were too many foci. One could obtain perhaps as high a proportion as one focus per 50 lymphocytes placed on the membrane. It was clear that, if this had been an immune response comparable to antibody production, where we assumed that there must be something more than 10^4 distinct immune patterns, the figures did not make sense. Either the clonal selection dogma of one cell, one immune pattern, was wrong, or some other set of processes was concerned. To my considerable relief, the second alternative has now become acceptable, though opinion on how it should be formulated is far from uniform. Probably everyone is agreed that, whatever the reaction's form, it is in some way associated with the major histocompatibility antigens and that the genes that control the mechanism are closely linked to those that code for these antigens in mice, and presumably in man.

In my first chapter, I outlined how I thought the vertebrate immune system may have evolved, and I shall recapitulate and elaborate part of that approach in the present context. Essentially, I assume that the whole immune system, based on surface proteins of lymphocytes and other mobile cells, has evolved from intercellular recognition units that were originally a self-self recognition mechanism helping to maintain the structure of metazoan organisms. Almost certainly it had the character of a $\beta 2$ microglobulin, which in various forms has a function in both major histocompatibility antigens and immunoglobulins. I also assume that representative structures from at least three of the stages of evolution have persisted.

1. Katz et al. (1973) find that effective cooperation between T and B cells is possible only when both sets of cells are from mice of the same pure strain. This presumably requires mutual recognition by some surface protein equivalent to the simplest intercellular recognition mechanism.

2. The allelic recognition mechanism, which I expressed as Aa, Bb, Cc . . . , includes, by hypothesis, the major histocompatibility antigens (MHCA's) and the histocompatibility, or allogeneic, receptors (AR's). Having due regard for the fact that four gene products from two loci give rise to an MHCA, we can still simplify discussion by signifying it with a single letter. All the cells in an individual that carry the MHCA on their surface have the same complex antigen, B, for example. Since all genetically distinct individuals recognize B as foreign, we must assume that in a B individual there are lymphocytes with all receptors, a, c, d, e, . . . , needed to recognize any type but B. Simply by analogy with the immunoglobulin system, one assumes that each cell carries only one AR and develops clonally. The receptor is presumably protein and is not immunoglobulin, but nothing more definite is available about its chemical structure. It is the simplest postulate that all T lymphocytes that carry an MHCA will be equipped with an AR, and that, when contact occurs with the corresponding MHCA, the various lymphokine capacities of the cell will be brought into play.

To be specific, this mechanism is held primarily responsible for graft-versus-host reactions like the one on the chorioallantoic membrane and for mixed lymphocyte reactions. It is also important in regard to homograft rejection reactions.

3. The immunoglobulin system is of course much more versatile than the allelic recognition mechanism and has already been extensively discussed. It must be recognized that the Ig system is omnicompetent and is capable of developing antibody or "armed" T cells against any organic configuration. This will include alloge-

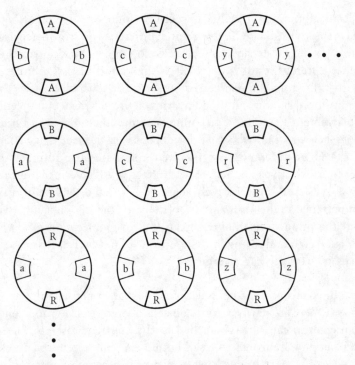

FIGURE 3–1. *Possible relationships of allogeneic reactions between lymphocytes from different members of the same species. The capital letters (A, B, and R) represent major histocompatibility antigens; the lower-case letters designate the hypothetical receptors with which they react.*

neic cells and any of their surface components that can be recognized as foreign, not only the major histocompatibility antigens, but also any minor antigenic difference, from what is present in the cells of the recipient individual. From this angle it is of special interest to note Simonsen's findings in regard to graft-versus-host reactions in mice (1962). If leucocytes from a mouse of MHCA "B" are injected intravenously into another mouse of a different MHCA, "M," the index of graft-versus-host action (the degree of enlargement of the spleen) will have a high and relatively constant value. The result will not be changed if the donor, B, is immunized with M cells, a procedure that would be expected to increase the number of specifically armed T cells. However, if donor and recipient both have the same MHCA but have minor differences that are detectable —e.g., by relatively slow mutual rejection of crossed skin grafts—a quite different result is obtained. If the donor, B1, is immunized with cells from the recipient strain, B2, the leucocytes from the immunized donor will produce a much greater degree of splenic enlargement than leucocytes from the normal animal. The difference between the two situations depends on the fact that, where the MHCA differences are involved, there are large numbers of specifically active lymphocytes with effective AR's. A small increase in T cells carrying a passively acquired Ig receptor will be of little importance. In the B1/B2 situation, however, the AR is not effective, but the minor foreign antigen can lead to proliferation of appropriate B cells and, by hypothesis, arming of newly differentiated T cells in relatively large numbers.

This concept, that neutral T cells can be armed appropriately only if there are newly activated B cells liberating IgM or its monomeric form, can now be applied to the apparent discrepancy in Warner and Szenberg's study of hormonally bursectomized chickens (1961). Most immunologists accept a tuberculin reaction or the accelerated response to vaccinia in an immune subject as being based on T cell responses. Yet the bursectomized chickens failed to give either reaction. If our hypothesis is correct, this is precisely what would be expected, since the absence of B cells would provide no source of immunoglobulin to arm T cells with the Ig receptors necessary.

At this point too we can go back to the problem of the range of immune responses shown by patients with congenital agammaglobulinemia, particularly their ability to deal normally with measles and several other viral infections. If, as seems to be generally accepted, we take the essential functional lesion to be the inability of B cells to mature to plasma cells, it is possible to explain the very low levels but never complete absence of IgM by the presence of such B cells, and to explain the capacity of the immune system to react in normal fashion with measles and vaccinia by assuming that

T cells are normal and can be armed passively from stimulated B cells of appropriate specificity.

I now come to what seems to me the main justification for this point of view: the ease with which it explains the rapid recruitment of cells when they are needed in an emergency and provides a means of equipping them with the right weapons. If, as is the standard opinion, T cells develop their specific immune pattern of immunoglobulin in the same way as B cells, but independently, it is very difficult to see how, in the early stages of an immune response, B and T cells of essentially the same specificity will ever be able to find themselves in close proximity in the right place at the right time. If, however, the B cell is the primary producer of all specific pattern in immunoglobulin, we have a much more economical and logical situation. It is well known that when hypersensitivity to tuberculin is transferred to a normal guinea pig by large numbers of lymphocytes (necessarily both B and T) from a tuberculous animal, suitable experiments show that there are only a few of the donor cells present in the cellular infiltrate at the challenge site. The vast majority are host cells that have only recently been produced.

The simplest interpretation could be that the mixed population of cells from the tuberculin-sensitive donor contains a proportion of specifically reactive T and B cells as well as antigens derived from tubercle bacilli. In the interaction with the recipient's immune system, and among the donor cells, lymphokines will be liberated and a variety of cellular changes, including the allogeneic effect of Katz et al. (1973), set in train. Activation of B cells and the appearance of large numbers of newly formed donor T cells will allow passive arming of the latter, which will then provide most of the cells that accumulate in the delayed hypersensitivity reactions—positive tuberculin tests—when the passively sensitized guinea pigs are challenged.

In active sensitization, in any draining lymph node there will be an accumulation of B cells reactive with the antigenic determinants concerned, and once these start proliferating monomeric IgM will leak and be available to arm the simultaneously proliferating T cells. This would provide a magnificent way to recruit large numbers of T cells of the *right* immune specificity to assist in whatever needs to be done. Such an interpretation also explains Morris's fetal thymectomy experiments. What is lacking in the treated lambs during their first months of postnatal life is the massive population of thymus-derived T cells uncommitted in regard to any Ig specificity.

Although this hypothesis seems reasonably plausible, it has a number of features that, if tested experimentally, might be proved wrong. If it is invalidated, I have no doubt that in the process something better than either the nebulous present-day consensus opinion, or this too imaginative picture that I have been enthusiastically painting, will emerge.

And that is what biological science is all about.

A HOMEOSTATIC AND SELF-MONITORING IMMUNE SYSTEM

Since the days of Claude Bernard in the nineteenth century, physiologists have recognized the homeostatic quality of all bodily systems. The objective seems to be the maintenance of the stability of the body so that all the needs of life are fulfilled. For example, whenever violent exercise temporarily disturbs almost every metabolic parameter, the subsequent period of rest and relaxation automatically restores the bodily systems to normal. In many ways the immune mechanism is the homeostatic system par excellence.

It is dangerous to say that any biological system is more complex than another; one has only to read a good review of some area of biology other then one's own to realize how vastly more intricate is the reality than the working picture one has accepted in the past. So it is only tentatively that I claim that the immune system is second only to the nervous system in the intricacy of the mechanisms by which it watches and maintains control over the integrity of the mobile cells of the blood and lymph circulations. In the process, the system must always be on a 24-hour alert to combat foreign intrusions as well as "disloyalty" from within. To pursue the political analogy further, one of the chief functions of the system is to maintain a series of checks and counterchecks against inappropriate action by its own agents. The system is necessarily complex, first because of the difficulty of distinguishing self from not-self, of knowing who is in his proper place, and who, if unchecked, will endanger the safety of the organism. Another formidable difficulty derives from the way in which specificity—the capacity to recognize—can only arise in a random fashion.

I have found Jacques Monod's book, *Chance and Necessity*, most impressive, and I have paraphrased its central theme to bring to light its relevance to immunity. It is that nature (or evolution) can find no other way to introduce novelty than to produce in some wholly random fashion a wide diversity of inheritable pattern and then to expose those patterns to the test of selective survival. It is just Darwinism generalized to make it as applicable to microorganisms and to the mobile cells of the body as to the macroscopically visible plants and animals known in Darwin's day. To recapitulate briefly my remarks about clonal selection, we find the subgenes responsible for the L and H variable chains subject, during development, to a randomization procedure that is concentrated on the DNA that codes for the hypervariable regions. As in all such genetic processes, the informational changes produced in these regions are wholly random in character. The ultimate product is the complex configuration produced by the juxtaposition of L and H variable regions to form the combining site of antibody or immune receptor. Any such configurations that are of immediate potential value to the organism will be selected by intruding antigen for proliferation and/or antibody production. It will be equally evident that many of these randomly produced combining sites will be reactive against antigens or antigenic determinants present in the body, and are therefore unwanted and potentially dangerous.

At this point I should interpolate something about the expressions "antigen" and "antigenic determinant." Strictly speaking, they are applicable only to substances or submolecular atomic groupings that can cause the appearance of antibodies in the particular kind of animal being considered, and that can react with those antibodies. It is almost axiomatic therefore that the proteins and other macromolecular constituents of the body are nonantigenic. Nevertheless, almost all of them can be shown to be antigenic in some other species of animal, and many of them by special manipulations—usually of the sort one calls unbiological—can be antigenic in animals of their own type. So I shall speak not infrequently of antigenic determinants, even when referring to the reacting animal's own constituents, and define an antigenic determinant (AD) as any chemical configuration that reacts, i.e., unites noncovalently, with the combining site of an antibody or immune receptor with high enough affinity to allow the occurrence of union to be demonstrated.

The first requirement for an effective immune system is to ensure that immunocytes bearing immune patterns that unite too readily with accessible AD's in the body shall be eliminated or prevented from proliferating. I have no doubt whatever that this is effectively achieved, but I have become less and less certain about *how* it is achieved. One of my colleagues told me a year or two ago that he had listed 24 different ways by which an animal could be rendered nonreactive—i.e., tolerant—against an antigen it would normally react with. Many of those had no bearing on the problem of natural tolerance—why an animal, which under abnormal conditions *can* react damagingly against some of its own thousands of potential antigens to give autoimmune disease, in the overwhelming majority of individuals never does so. There is one very useful general statement due to Avrion Mitchison—that tolerance results whenever an antigen can be maintained constantly present and accessible in the animal—but this tells nothing about the mechanisms involved.

What can be taken as certain is that T cells are more important than B cells in the development of tolerance, and for a long time I had a very satisfying picture, based on the assumption (which still may be correct) that all T cells developed in the thymus by synthesizing their own IgMl receptors, and that most of them died before or soon after leaving the thymus, as a result of reacting too actively with a "self" antigenic determinant on some accessible body component. If the alternative I favor now of passive arming of T cells is correct, this could still take place if there were ways by which small amounts of IgM randomly mixed could reach the cells maturing in the thymus. What seems to be reasonably certain is that T cells are much more easily made tolerant, i.e., in one way or another rendered immunologically invisible, than B cells. B cells with some capacity to react with self components of all sorts appear to be always available, but in the absence of corresponding T cells, proliferation, production of antibody, and maturation to plasma cells does not take place. B cells can be made nonresponsive in various ways, but it is uncertain what part this plays in natural tolerance.

The diagram in Figure 4-1 may be helpful for understanding these matters, but, like so many theoretical aspects of current immunology, it could be regarded by many competent people as unproven and inadequate to explain some aspect of immunology with which they have had experience. It is an attempt to plot what happens to a T or B cell at various stages of maturity when it encounters an antigenic determinant (AD) that can make an effective union with the combining site of a cell's Ig receptor. Now it is obvious that what happens will depend on: (1) the degree of affinity of AD for combining site; (2) the concentration of AD in the immediate neighborhood of the cell surface; (3) how long that concentration is maintained. It seems reasonable to assume that the effect on the cell will be proportional to some function incorporating all three factors, which we can represent as f Sp, i.e., the specific component. In addition to this, an immunocyte can also be influenced by nonspecific mitogens such as phytohemagglutinin or bacterial lipopolysaccharide, and by the mitogens liberated from helper T cells by

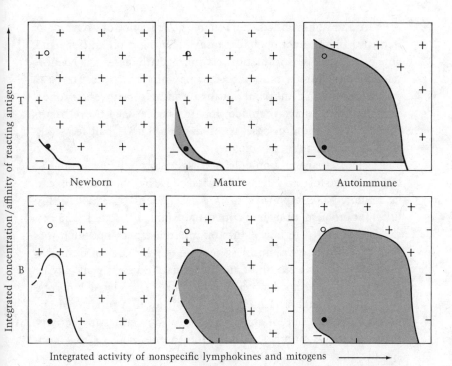

FIGURE 4–1. *The different susceptibility of freshly differentiated (new-born), mature, and autoimmune (resistant) T and B lymphocytes to initial contact with specific antigen. The minus signs signify no reaction; shaded areas indicate proliferation and functional activity; plus signs indicate death or inhibition of activity.*

specific contact but acting essentially nonspecifically on adjacent B cells. There are probably more of these nonspecific stimulants to immunocyte activation, but in any given situation it should also be possible to combine them as f N-Sp, as the nonspecific component. In the figure, f Sp is plotted as ordinate, f N-Sp as abscissae, and three areas are delimited by lines. In the clear area, less than 50 percent of the cells are affected in any way; in the shaded area, more than 50 percent are activated to proliferate, synthesize antibody, liberate lymphokines, or develop cytotoxicity; in the area marked with daggers, more than 50 percent are rendered nonviable. In other words, the contention is that as one increases the impact of these specific and nonspecific factors there is a sequence of no effect, of activation and functional response including proliferation, and, finally, of excessive stimulation leading to death of the cell. I believe that it is a type of diagram that, with appropriate modifications, can be quite useful in thinking about any immunological problem one is puzzling over. I have included, for instance, what I think occurs when autoimmune disease arises in man, but I shall leave discussion of that to a later chapter.

I regret that I cannot provide any satisfactory general account of either natural tolerance or of the various ways by which animals can be rendered nonresponsive to foreign antigens; it is a basically different problem, though of course not wholly unrelated. All I can say is that there are many different circumstances in which it is necessary for the immune system to render an immunocyte ineffective for one reason or another. That "no go" signal may be given in several forms. The cell may be lethally stimulated. It may be stimulated in such a fashion that it matures to a functional but nonproliferating cell, or some other means of inhibiting activity may be used—a number of inhibitory agents, specific and nonspecific, have been observed in one or another experimental situation.

Every year or two, some new complexity comes into the picture; at present, suppressor T cells are in fashion. In various ways one can obtain populations of lymphocytes that are capable of suppressing the activity of an immunocyte population either in producing antibody or is some form of cell-mediated immunity. Then, since 1972 certain complexities have been brought into tumor immunity: i.e., we can have cell-mediated immunity blocked by antibody and sometimes the blocking antibody inhibited by a nonspecific serum inhibitor.

These complications are unfortunate, but I cannot honestly provide anything that is attractively simple and yet basically true. Biology has been growing up rapidly in the last two or three decades, and immunology at least as fast as any other biological discipline. I am sure that Jerne is right, that the time is due for a new conceptual "great leap forward," what Kuhn calls a new paradigm that will incorporate clonal selection but provide a wider framework of ideas on which to start building again. Jerne (1971) has made a brilliant start on a "network theory," using as its basis the concept of *idiotype*, which I have not yet mentioned. It is not an easy concept to explain, but I shall do my best.

Both antibodies and receptors on immunocyte surfaces are accessible to other antibodies and receptors on other immunocytes. In principle, an antibody or a receptor could function as an antigen if it could stimulate a cell with an appropriate receptor. Now if you think of what I said about the origin of the diversity of antibody patterns, particularly of Baltimore's TDT approach (see p. 24), you will realize that the hypervariable region, particularly two stably oriented hypervariable regions, represents a genetically abnormal AD, a peptide configuration alien to those produced by normal genetic processes. The specific combining site, in other words, is a potential antigenic determinant, and when it functions as such it is called, in Jerne's nomenclature, an idiotope. The nature of the anti-antibody produced defines its idiotype. Experimentally, it seems to be established that whenever an adequate amount of a single antibody is produced in or injected into an animal, anti-idiotypic sera are produced. The anti-idiotypic antibody will in turn have its specific idiotope, giving rise to the possibility of an infinite series of anti-anti-antibodies, anti-anti-anti-antibodies, and so on. In fact, the situation may become even more interesting. I have said that any organic configuration A can be matched in complementary steric fashion by a peptide combining site on an antibody a. Little a can be regarded as a mirror image of big A, and if we now make an antibody against a, its mirror image should be identical immunologically to A. There are some experiments that support this possibility. I suspect that we will have to represent the situation, not by the infinite series of reflections seen in a pair of bright and strictly parallel mirrors, but by what could be seen if the mirrors had a slightly frosted and not completely plane surface, so that A^1 was at a very much lower intensity than A and somewhat distorted, whereas A^2 was hardly discernible. The same would hold for a^1 and a^2. You can see the sort of complications that might arise when real antigen

A and equivalent antigens A^1 and A^2 of the same specificity are present in the system.

An interesting development of idiotype work that is very relevant to this interpretation appeared late in 1973 from Rowley's laboratory in Chicago (Rowley et al., 1973). It is now well known that certain mouse myeloma proteins are essentially monoclonal antibodies reacting specifically with phosphorylcholine haptens. A variety of artificial antigens and some types of pneumococcal antigens carry the phosphorylcholine hapten and will induce antibody with the same idiotype as the standard myeloma protein TEPC 15. They produced in mice an anti-idiotype antiserum, which they refer to as antireceptor antibody (ARA). If you examine Figure 4-1, you will realize that the antibody configuration of ARA should be equivalent to the configuration of phosphorylcholine hapten and should be capable also of reacting similarly with the receptors of immunocytes capable of recognizing phosphorylcholine.

They injected ARA into neonatal mice and into two-month-old mice, and at appropriate times subsequently tested both types of experimental animal and controls of similar age for their capacity to produce specific plaque-forming cells four days after challenge with a potent phosphorylcholine antigen. The results were as one might expect. The neonatally injected mice showed approximately 0.3 percent of control plaque-forming cells at three months, and at eight months about 4.5 percent: i.e., tolerance was long-lasting and nearly complete. Mice injected with ARA at two months showed an unresponsiveness of short duration, with about 2 percent response to eight days' challenge that rapidly rose to 80 percent by four weeks.

Other studies were made to detect immunocytes capable of reacting with phosphorylcholine with the use of normal untreated mice and two groups treated with antireceptor antibody. The first was injected neonatally and tested at two months of age, the second group injected at two months of age and tested a week later. All three groups had no anti-phosphorylcholine antibody. The normal mice showed 20 to 30 active cells per 10^4 spleen cells. Both other groups were negative, but by incubation at 37 degrees and repeated washing, the third group eventually showed about 20 per 10^4 with fluorescence. In other words, neonatal cells capable of reaction were killed or permanently deleted, whereas cells in mature mice of appropriate specificity were reversibly inactivated for a short period.

In some ways these experiments can be regarded as showing how Jerne's ideas on idiotopes could allow means of controlling immune activity. It is unlikely, however, that neonatal tolerance is normally mediated, as Rowley and his Chicago coworkers suggested, by this particular mechanism.

I won't try to go any further in elaborating this *eigen* system of Jerne (1976), but I am convinced the immune system is really much more complicated. And to be slightly paradoxical, I shall try to persuade you that only by grasping this complexity is it possible to build up a reasonably simple and useful way of thinking about it.

In the course of this book I have discussed many types of specifically reactive molecules or parts of molecules. They include immunoglobulins, inhibitors, and lymphokines in solution, and, on the surface of lymphocytes, Ig receptors, major histocompatibility antigens (MHCA's), allogeneic receptors, and no doubt many others. On the surface of macrophages are receptors to which IgG can be attached and an incompletely known mechanism by which antigens are associated with macrophages or dendritic phagocytic cells in lymphoid tissue. Lymphocytes have receptors for the active lectins phytohemagglutinin and concanavallin A, whose normal functions are unknown, as well as receptors for hormones such as insulin and cortisol. In addition we must not forget that the lymphokines produced by T cells on antigenic or other types of stimulation are macromolecular, and presumably proteins of specifically determined structure acting on equally specific receptors on the cells they influence.

Let us now look at some of the requirements for effective functioning of the immune system, keeping in mind not only the various ways in which immunopathological conditions can arise but also normal physiological requirements. I have already discussed the need for recognizing fine differences in chemical structure that differentiate self from not-self. Here I want to point out two or three situations in which it is necessary to provide secondary controls to prevent too facile a recognition of foreignness doing inadmissible damage. The first example is the response to pregnancy in which a source of foreign paternal antigens is implanted in the tissues of the mother. There are paternal antigens, particularly the major histocompatibility antigens, against which immune responses, usually antibody production, can often be detected after a series of pregnancies. Much experimental work has been done on the mechanisms that minimize damage, such as the nonimmunogenic quality of the trophoblast, the only fetal tissue that makes immediate contact with the cells and fluids of the mother, and, of course, on the diagnosis and treatment of Rh disease and other rarer examples of how things may go wrong. Another set of somewhat similar difficulties arises when we consider the scavenging problems of the body—how to eliminate worn out and damaged red cells or the debris that must be cleared away after each episode of local trauma and infection; and, of very direct interest to the immunologist, how to deal with immunoglobulin antibody denatured by contact with antigen or to dispose of cytotoxic T cells irretrievably damaged in the exercise of their function. Without attempting to elaborate the detail in any specific example, it is surely evident once again how refined the control must be to resolve such problems.

The next point to be considered is the frequency, particularly in childhood, with which the immune system must respond to the major emergency of a severe systemic infection calling for the rapid mobilization of B and T cells with hyperactive production of antibody. Often, as in measles at the height of the rash, massive production of lymphokines and extensive destruction of lymphocytes occur. The system must combat such episodes effectively but without letting down the guard against other possible emergencies that may arise simultaneously. Great flexibility is required, as in what can be called a "fail-safe" system, by which, if one mechanism is overwhelmed or inactivated, another can—at least temporarily—provide adequate reserve function.

By the phrase "a self-monitoring system" (included in the title of this chapter), I mean that it is a necessary function that lymphocytes showing qualities that could menace survival must be recognized and eliminated or rendered harmless. There have been some implicit mentions of this already, but it is necessary to say something more specifically. A very popular theme for experimental study since 1973 has been suppressor T cells; there are several situations in which administration of a suitable subpopulation of lymphocytes inhibits immune responses, either of antibody production or of some manifestation of cell-mediated immunity. Here we must have the two functions of recognition and elimination or inhibition in action against B and T cell subpopulations respectively; each presumably provides an example of a biologically significant process of self-monitoring. The most important indication, however, of the importance of self-monitoring comes from the observation that, in humans under prolonged immunosuppression or suffering from one of the subacute or partially controllable immunodeficiency diseases, such as ataxia telangiectasia, malignant disease of lymphocytes is much more frequent than in normal populations. There is a significant increase as well in other types of malignant disease, but in all groups the relative excess is much greater in the so-called lymphoreticular tumors, most of which are probably derived from B cells. In kidney-transplant patients under continuing immunosuppressive drugs, the incidence of such tumors is 350 times what it would be in a comparable control population. If one analyzes the situation, the only logical interpretation seems to be that lymphocytes are rather unduly prone to malignant change but that if the immune system is functioning normally the surveillance or self-monitoring system is extremely effective. For reasons I shall discuss in chapter 8 it is likely that a similar control may be exercised over lymphocytes that have become capable of initiating autoimmune disease.

From all these perspectives, then, we arrive at a concept of the immune system as a homeostatic and self-monitoring unit with a control system reminiscent of the computerized control of a modern petrochemical complex with its sensors constantly monitoring for change in vital parameters and automatically calling positive or negative feedback mechanisms into action. The immunological controls differ from this computerized control in their flexibility and their need to respond to major calamities as well as to the minor fluctuations in average functioning, and control is of course limited to processes that are possible with biological material. I like to think of this system as an immensely complex interacting network of mobile lymphocytes comprising thousands of distinguishable subpopulations. Control involves the impact of patterned macromolecules, carrying genetically coded information, on receptors they can recognize and, depending on circumstances, can stimulate to give synthesizing, proliferative, or destructive signals to the cell.

The whole structure of the blood and lymph circulations and of the peripheral lymphoid tissues and the processes by which lymphocytes move from one compartment to another, work together to ensure the highest likelihood that any lymphocyte may make a tentative contact with any other lymphocyte and learn whether there are possibilities of mutual recognition and reaction. The general lymphocyte circulation is replenished by proliferations of cells in thymus and bone marrow and in the germinal centers, diffuse lymphoid tissue in spleen, lymph nodes, and various accumulations of lymphoid tissue along the gastrointestinal tract. In general, new cells will pass via lymph vessels into the thoracic duct and from there into the circulating blood. From the general capillary circulation, many move into the tissues, particularly of the gut wall, and are collected from there by afferent lymphatics to the lymph nodes. Others pass actively into lymphoid tissue from the blood by passing through the cuboidal endothelial cells of postcapillary venules in lymphoid tissue. Lymphocytes are actively motile, and in the lymph nodes one can picture a dynamic situation in which cells move constantly in all directions but the general trend is from the peripheral sinuses toward the collecting vessels of the hilum. In life it would probably appear as a writhing "bag of worms," with more stable regions in the germinal centers and in the medullary cords with their plasma cells. In the sheep, a popliteal lymph node can be cannulated in both afferent and efferent trunks, and it is possible, by infusing antigen into the afferent channel and collecting everything that emerges from the efferent, to show that *all* reactive lymphocytes specific for the antigen in the whole of the body can be trapped in that lymph node. If, after a week, the experiment is terminated by excising the lymph node with its cannulated vessels, the animal can be shown to contain neither antigen nor reactive cells. Immunologically, it has been reconstituted as a virgin animal in regard to that particular antigen. One could hardly have a more striking demonstration of the point I am making—that every lymphocyte has an opportunity to make contact with every other lymphocyte, and that in this fashion countless effective interactions result that mediate the homeostasis and self-monitoring quality of the system.

The situation is unique in the intensely heterogeneous population of cells capable of highly specific interactions among subpopulations without the necessity of any physical segregation. I can think of no form of human technology that even remotely resembles it. Within the system an ongoing transfer of an appropriate reaction to information occurs in much the same sense as it does in the central nervous system. There, however, we have a clearly demarcated, spatially structured system of circuitry as a basis for information transfer. Much more than circuitry is involved, but that at least is something we can imitate in principle with the microcircuits of our computers. The only possible analogies of the immune system are biological ones. The traffic of the lymphocytes, even as demonstrated under the coverslip by accelerated film sequences, reminds me of the interchanges one sees on the landing board of a beehive in summer or the movement among workers on and around an ants' nest when a food source is being exploited. And without too great an effort of the imagination, it is possible to extend the analogy to the activity that occurs on the floor of the stock exchanges of the world in boom or panic times.

To return to the immune system, at the functional level one can conceive of it only as a multidimensional universe presenting quite extraordinary difficulties for its effective understanding. There is no particular difficulty in devising experiments, and provided the conditions are rigidly standardized, reproducible results will be obtained. Yet most of those "good" experiments are best considered as making no more than two-dimensional sections of a multidimensional universe. I find myself forever reminding my colleagues and myself that the sine qua non for a definitive biological experiment—working with genetically uniform organisms or cells— just cannot from the very nature of the subject be applied to immunology. All that can be hoped for is that each new experiment will test a cross-section different from all the previous ones and make some conclusion a little more likely. My pessimism about the difficulties notwithstanding, I invariably find that anything I have written more than a year previously is outdated in some point or other, and I expect that this is likely to continue for the foreseeable future.

I seem to have reached a rather gloomy conclusion, but, as I promised, I think that something cheerful may be derived from it. I am going to conclude this discussion by trying to assess what we seek in studying immunology as an aspect of normal body function, and how far we have come by 1975.

The first objective in a serious approach to immunology should be to obtain a broad understanding, with a minimum of detail, of how immunology fits into the pattern of biology—of the way in which the immune system evolved, its function and coordination with other body systems, and its development from the embryo onwards. At the same time, such an outline should provide an adequate background for easy application of immunological ideas to the detail of practical immunological work in public health, clinical, and veterinary practice.

Such an approach, however, is quite inadequate as a background for new exploratory investigation. I believe that the essential question that needs asking is how the increasing mass of good experimental work now being published is to be made effective use of.

To begin with, it may be helpful if I try to enumerate briefly the significant features of immunology that can be accepted as established and to a considerable extent understood.

1. The immune system, in association with other processes, takes a major part in terminating infectious disease and in preventing or cutting short any subsequent infection by the same agent. Arising out of the recognition of this function are the various diagnostic procedures based on immune responses and the use of vaccines, living or killed, to imitate subclinical infection.

2. Immune mechanisms exist to ensure that cells of genetically different character that have been introduced into or arise in the body are recognized as foreign and rejected. This concept of the difference between self and not-self is fundamental, but most of the unsolved problems of immunology emerge when we attempt to look to its consequences. These include the evolutionary origin of vertebrate immunity, the existence and, if it exists, the nature of the allogeneic recognition mechanism and its relation to the major histocompatibility antigens, the mechanism by which natural (intrinsic) tolerance to body components is developed and maintained, and the quite closely related ways in which nonresponsiveness to foreign antigens can be induced. This last consequence is, of course, of great importance for the transplantation of kidneys and other organs or tissues.

3. Also established is the clonal selection approach to the production of antibody by B cells and, with appropriate qualifications, to the proliferation of T cells.

4. Probably the best understood segment of immunology is the nature of immunoglobulins—the means by which they have evolved, their genetic control and the processes in the somatic genome by which an immense diversity of pattern capable of reacting with any organic configuration can be provided.

5. The T cells are definable essentially as cells that can manifest immune responses, but they are not known to synthesize and secrete significant amounts of immunoglobulin antibodies. It is clear that they are important in controlling the activity of immune responses and in producing for this and other purposes a variety of pharmacologically active lymphokines. The unresolved difficulties in their understanding have been extensively discussed in chapter 3. I am not wholly convinced that the division into B and T cells is more than a provisional one, nor do I feel it has yet made any significant impact on clinical medicine.

6. The concept of the immune system as a homeostatic and self-monitoring functional structure, an *eigen* system in Jerne's terms, is what I have tried to depict in this chapter. In chapters 6 and 8 I hope to indicate how important this concept is for the understanding of autoimmune disease and the pathology of the immune system in old age. I would emphasize again that it is essential to the immune system's function that the immunocyte populations should be heterogeneous, a condition thereby making rigid analysis by the standard scientific approach basically impossible.

That brings me to my final question in this chapter. How is the mass of work in immunology that has been published since the 1950s and will be published in the immediate future to be made and kept accessible? The answer may well be that the question as phrased implies a rather naive view of the nature of experimental research in any complex biological field. The productive worker in immunology is the person who has concentrated on a specific field and a well defined approach. He is completely in command of his own system and may have very little interest outside it, apart from any reports that impugn the validity of his conclusions or indicate a new approach directly applicable to his own system. His work becomes of importance to immunologists outside his special field only when he can produce some general statement that has some significance for immunology as a whole—something that must be introduced into any set of lectures on the contemporary state of the art and be incorporated into the next edition of all good undergraduate texts. One has only to make a graph of the dates of publication of references quoted in a dozen 1974 papers to realize that, once a new finding of that significance has emerged, only a year or two is required to confirm its validity and to make plausible applications to other systems. Thereafter the papers are never looked at again by active workers. I can imagine that it could be a very useful exercise for a first-rate worker to survey the field of, say, T and B cell differentiation and decide from hindsight what would seem to have been the best strain of animal and the best set of antigens to use. If he then assembled a highly competent team and used the best modern technique to repeat all the significant experiments since 1960, he would probably clarify many doubtful points and produce a definitive set of comparable data to which human logic and computer expertise could be profitably applied. Even then, I doubt whether logical analysis of that multidimensional universe would be extended much further than it already has been.

And, if I know anything of the psychology of research, such an exercise never will be undertaken.

MUTATION

MUTATION MEANS CHANGE. In its biological sense it refers to a rarely occurring and apparently random change by which an organism or a cell undergoes an abrupt change in some observable character. The change is passed on to descendants in a fashion that points to the mutation being dependent on a change in the nucleotide sequence of a DNA segment. The word mutation is a tricky one that needs to be watched carefully. With the exception of professional geneticists, probably most people with a reasonable knowledge of biology would say that a mutation is a result of damage to DNA, usually by nuclear radiation and the like, or by some chemical mutagen. My contention will be that this is a very incomplete statement and basically a wrong one. However, some discussion leading up to that point will be necessary, and I should like to begin by recalling something about how DNA is replicated and repaired. I am not really a geneticist, and I am certainly a year or two behind the growing edge, but with the help of Watson's *Molecular Biology of the Gene* and some recent reviews I hope to avoid serious mistakes.

In the nucleus of each human somatic cell (diploid) there are about 6,000 million nucleotide pairs in the cell's DNA. The process by which these are replicated at each cell generation is one that quite transcends technology. A good proportion of that DNA is probably redundant in some sense, but even if only one-tenth is fully functional DNA, that capacity to handle billions of accurate nucleotide insertions within an hour or two during mitosis still remains fantastic. We know a good deal about viral and bacterial DNA replication, but in eukaryotic cells (including mammalian cells) there is virtually no way in which the visible behavior of the chromosomes can be correlated with what is going on at the molecular level. It is probably true to say that in mammalian cells replication of DNA takes place over many short segments that must be incised, unwound, and, when the appropriate nucleotides are inserted, relinked into the system. In addition to the template function of the parental DNA strands, an elaborate array of enzymes must be functioning efficiently to maintain accuracy of the replicating patterns. Mammalian cells are undoubtedly more complex than bacteria, which are known to have at least eight enzymes involved in replication and repair of DNA. In vertebrate cells there are almost certainly more; all that can be said is that all the types of enzyme known from bacteria are represented in the higher forms. This makes it reasonable to use the bacterial findings as a simplified model for what probably occurs in eukaryotes.

It may be helpful to insert a summary of recent work from Arthur Kornberg's laboratory at Stanford University on the situation in *E. coli* (Schekman et al., 1974). In brief, replication of DNA requires, first, an unwinding protein, then the insertion by an RNA polymerase III of a short RNA segment as a primer. This initial stage varies according to the phage being used, and in all probability replication of the *E. coli* chromosome itself requires five distinct proteins for this phase. Insertion of nucleotides in proper sequence during the elongation phase is the responsiblity of DNA polymerase III, and this may be the key enzyme concerned in determining fidelity of pattern. Finally, the RNA primer must be excised, the gaps filled by DNA polymerase I, and the sequence sealed by the enzyme ligase. It is important to recognize how inseparable replication and repair processes are, and to realize that when one refers to DNA polymerase, this is merely shorthand for a very elaborate complex concerned with both functions.

Mutation results when some error arising in the course of DNA replication and repair produces a demonstrable and inheritable change in the descendants of the affected cell. In most discussion of mutation it is conventional to concentrate on those mutations whose expression is associated with and essentially due to change in the amino acid sequence of the gene product involved, usually an enzyme. This, however, restricts the mutational process to structural genes that code for a specific protein, though it is known that a substantial part of the DNA must have other functions. In recent years there has been much interest in the possiblity of mutations involving the "repetitive DNA" that appears to be responsible for control of the timing of gene activation or inhibition and other processes within the genome. It is not known how that control is exercised, but it is almost certainly *not* by the conventional gene product. Any discussion of mutation solely at the level of structural genes must be read with this qualification in mind.

An amino acid sequence change in a mutant enzyme indicates that the nucleotide sequence of the gene responsible for the protein has undergone a corresponding change but is otherwise biochemically and physiologically normal. It is not a damaged gene but one in which the informationally significant sequence has been altered.

There is a certain regularity in the occurrence of mutation that can be studied in detail in bacteria or bacterial viruses and indirectly from human statistics of genetic abnormalities or the incidence of diseases associated with somatic mutation. A certain *rate* of mutation is characteristic. It is possible that the frequency of mutation could have no cause, in the sense that it represented only the inescapable occurrence of error in the complex process of replication. However, as soon as it can be shown that the mutation rate can be raised or lowered from the standard rate by genetic or other changes, such a defeatist view must lapse. That the rate can in fact be altered can be demonstrated in the following ways:

1. In all organisms that have been studied, the mutation rate can be raised by large doses of X-rays or other type of ionizing radiation—200 roentgens (R) is the approximate amount required to double the rate with most organisms. Chromosome breakage is also observed, and appropriate experiment shows that breaks in DNA occur. Many chemical mutagens too, in addition to increasing the mutation rate, may also show evidence of DNA breakage and chromosomal abnormalities.

2. In the bacterial virus T4D, a large collection of mutants located to gene 43, which codes for a DNA polymerase, have been tested. The mutant strains include examples of greatly increased spontaneous mutation rate in the form of mutator strains. In these an increased mutation rate is evident for all the qualities that it is convenient to test. In addition, antimutator strains are also found, though less frequently; these show *diminished* mutations when the virus is exposed to a standard UV dose. The general mutation rate in an organism can therefore be raised or lowered by mutational change in the most important of the enzymes responsible for DNA replication and repair.

3. In most bacteria, appropriate treatment with manganous salts increases the mutation rate markedly without having the associated lethal effect shown by most mutagens. In short, the result is probably due to replacement of the zinc atom, which is an essential part of all DNA polymerases, by manganese, and to a consequent minor change in the enzyme configuration.

4. As I shall elaborate later, the human skin disease xeroderma pigmentosum produces large numbers of freckles and other skin lesions with the quality of somatic mutations. It is a Mendelian (autosomal recessive) condition and is known to be associated with inefficiency in the repair of DNA damaged by ultraviolet irradiation. This example, too, gives us good reason to attribute mutation to inefficiency in the replication or repair of DNA.

These observations are sufficient to justify looking for specific influences on mutation rate, and offer an a priori case for paying special attention to the process of repair of DNA after damage by physical or chemical mutagens. Also, as will be evident, the possibility that inefficiency in the enzymes concerned is responsible for most of the increases in mutation rates is very much in my mind. One may in fact almost summarize what I am going to discuss for the rest of this book as the implications of the concept of intrinsic mutagenesis—the hypothesis that mutation results from error produced in the course of replication and repair of DNA by DNA polymerases of varying degrees of error proneness.

The Significance of Physical and Chemical Mutagens

The advent of nuclear weapons and nuclear power has made the subject of mutation one of the most prominent sociomedical problems of the present day, and perhaps of equivalent concern is the fear that chemical mutagens are being unknowingly but inevitably introduced into the food, water, and air of our technological environment. In discussing those aspects of mutation that are relevant to the themes of these chapters, it is expedient for me to use, as much as possible, the most extensively studied and discussed system—the effect of ionizing radiation (X-rays and the α, β, γ, and neutron radiations from radioactive atoms and reactions) on man.

In such discussions it is almost universally accepted that ionizing radiation in a large enough dose can induce any type of germ-line mutation by damage to cells in the gonads, and any type of malignancy. Direct evidence of germ-line damage in the form of mutation has never been provided from human material. There is every reason, however, to suppose that all the Mendelian conditions we observe are derived, each from a germ-line mutation, at some time in previous generations and initially from a single cell. To obtain an assessment of human germ-line mutation rates, it is necessary to concentrate on autosomal dominant conditions. For most individual studies, an analysis of these conditions will conclusively indicate whether the genetic abnormality is the result of a new mutation or has been transmitted from one of the parents. In such a typical and well-known example as achondroplastic dwarfism, it is immediately evident that an achondroplastic child whose parents are normal must represent a *new* mutation. No doubt autosomal recessive mutations occur at approximately the same frequency as dominant ones, but there is no convenient way to assess their number. In the discussion in the National Academy's BEIR Report (1972), the calculated incidence of new dominant mutations was approximately 10,000 per million births. Attempts to calculate what might be produced by thirty years' experience of background and medical exposures gave widely divergent figures, varying from one-eighth to one-thousandth of the spontaneous rate.

For good practical reasons the incidence of leukemia (chronic myeloid and acute leukemia but not lymphatic leukemia) is taken as a yardstick for the extent of radiation-induced somatic mutation in man. There are some extensive and reliable data on the incidence of leukemia in patients with ankylosing spondylitis treated with heavy doses of X-rays, and a better estimate than usual can be made of the dose-effect relationship. Comparison of the spontaneous rate with that which might be calculated for fifty years of background radiation has indicated that other causes must have been responsible for 95 to 99 percent of the observed incidence in normal populations.

Since the calculated incidence both for autosomal dominant mutations and for leukemia is based on the assumption that the likelihood of damage is proportional to dose and that the lesion is irreversible, the "expected" values are almost certainly much too high. The lesions produced in DNA by ultraviolet or X-irradiation are subject to complex and very efficient repair processes—a fact that must be given much more weight now than in the past.

The first indication that any type of radiation damage to DNA was reversible came when it was found by Albert Kelner (1949) that bacterial viruses, apparently inactivated by ultraviolet, could be revived by exposure to visible light. This led to a concentration of interest on the nature of ultraviolet action and the processes by which that action could be prevented or reversed. Those studies have culminated in the finding by Cleaver (1969) that the skin lesions in the genetic disease xeroderma pigmentosum are associated with a well marked inefficiency in the repair of DNA lesions produced by ultraviolet light in fibroblasts cultured from such patients. The likelihood is high therefore that the characteristic skin lesions can be ascribed to somatic mutational errors generated by error-prone repair enzymes.

In discussing the nature of mutation therefore, it is best to concentrate on the effect of ultraviolet irradiation of bacteria, which is not only the microbial geneticist's favorite way to raise the mutation rate but also the best understood. The primary effect of ultraviolet is to cause a covalent chemical union between two adjacent thymine bases on the same strand. This thymine dimerization prevents replication of the DNA segment concerned, and unless it is dealt with, the affected cell cannot multiply and is effectively killed. The effect of visible light reactivation is a specialized short cut, and the repair process that is carried out in the dark is probably of more general significance. It is, I think, worth discussing in some detail. In any genome there seems to be a constant succession of monitoring endonucleases that move around all parts of the genome and that are coded to recognize certain abnormalities. It is not known whether they are the same nucleases that recognize the points at which replication must start, and, as far as I am aware, nothing is known of the mechanism that enables the recognition to take place. Once the recognition occurs, an incision on the 5' side of the lesion is made by the endonuclease. An exonuclease now takes over and removes the portion of the strand containing the dimer. Next comes a DNA polymerase, which, with the help of other enzymes, inserts appropriate nucleotides complementary to the nucleotide sequence in the unchanged strand. When the gap is completed, the 3′ end of the inserted sequence is fixed to the rest of the strand by a ligase, the final enzyme in the series.

If both strands are involved with dimers, a much more complex maneuver is necessary, called postreplication repair.

When a bacterial cell or a mammalian cell is irradiated with ultraviolet, several types of result may be experimentally observed by the use of appropriate techniques.

1. The cell may be killed, the observation being that when the cells are plated (cloned), fewer colonies are observed on the plates receiving irradiated cells.

2. A repair process goes on usually to completion; this is assessed by adding tritiated thymidine and comparing the rate of unscheduled DNA synthesis with standard cells. It can be measured either by scintillation counting or autoradiography.

3. Mutations are induced in the following cells: (a) somatic cells—in practice, the only mutations detectable are pigmented areas (freckles) and tumors arising in the skin; (b) in cells, bacterial or mammalian, being studied in culture—here a mutation is usually recognized by providing test plates containing some agent that will prevent all normal cells from growing but will allow a specific class of mutants to proliferate and produce colonies. The yield of colonies in terms of the number of cells plated will give the rate at which the particular mutant tested for arises.

It must be recognized that experiments of type 2 give quite different kinds of information from those of type 3; they tell nothing whatever about mutation. What they can tell is whether or not the process of repair at the chemical level can proceed at the normal rate as judged essentially by the speed with which new nucleotides are inserted by the active DNA polymerase. If it is delayed, this means that there are inefficiencies in the repair process, but it gives no information on how complete the repair is (it is only the insertion of nucleotides that is being measured) or on whether errors have been introduced into the nucleotide sequence when the repair is completed.

Recognition of mutation by either 3(a) or 3(b) has the implication that physical and functional repair is complete and allows the repeated occurrence of mitosis to produce a clone of descendent cells. The positive finding is that in the process, error has occurred in the nucleotide sequence, with a corresponding abnormality in the sequence of amino acid residues in the gene product.

The effect of ionizing radiation (X-rays, gamma rays, and the like) on DNA is mainly the breaking of strands, and the actual process of repair does not require the recognition and removal of a specific lesion like the thymine dimer. If there are deletions, gaps will have to be appropriately filled, and all the subsequent stages of repair are probably similar to that after ultraviolet damage. In studying mutation we are primarily interested in the way error can occur, in the sense that the sequence of nucleotides is changed, although functionally the whole genome is capable of normal mitosis. The errors will consist of single-base alteration, frame-shift mutations, or deletions. I shall not discuss the details of mechanism, but consider merely the conditions that could be expected to increase the rate of error formation in general.

On general grounds the number of errors should be influenced by three main factors. (1) Errors should be proportional to the amount of replication and repair required, perhaps measured by the number of nucleotides incorporated into new strands or portions thereof. (2) The number of errors should be a function of the complexity of the repair work needed. Mutations are known to be more common when postreplication repair is needed than when only single-strand lesions are present. It is also probable that certain sequences, such as a series of several nucleotides of the same type, are more prone to error than others. (3) Finally, the efficiency with which DNA polymerases and associated enzymes do their work must be of major influence.

The possibility or probability that simple thermal agitation induces the rare errors that lead to mutation seems unlikely. Loss of purine bases is apparently of quite frequent occurrence, but all cells contain a specific endonuclease capable of recognizing the loss, as well as the other enzymes required for rapid and complete repair.

Two other damaging effects of ionizing radiation have been extensively studied. The first is the production of chromosome breaks and secondary results such as translocations and other morphological abnormalities of the karyotype. A proportion of such cells of abnormal karyotype are capable of normal mitosis and not infrequently show a proliferative advantage over normal cells. Under certain circumstances, therefore, repair with error may be associated with abnormal chromosome morphology, which will often give vital help in following any clonal development of the mutant.

The second effect of administering large doses of X- or gamma-irradiation to mice or other animals is a shortening of lifespan with a generally equivalent speeding up of age-associated disease.

All four effects of ionizing radiation that are biologically recognizable—germ-line mutation, somatic mutation, chromosomal breakage or morphological abnormality, and shortening of lifespan—require quite large doses. To double the spontaneous rate of mutation in most situations requires a dose of the order of 200 R, which may be contrasted with the background radiation in a normal environment of 0.10 R per year, a total of 3 to 5 R for the period relevant to reproduction in man, or 7 R for the whole of life.

At this point we must face the necessity of supporting an unpopular conclusion, which has been expressed as follows in the BEIR Report (1972). "Exposure to man-made radiation below the level of background radiation will produce additional effects that are less in quantity and no different in kind from those which man has experienced and been able to tolerate throughout his history." It is generally accepted that there is no way of proving that background radiation has any effect at all in producing mutations, either germ-line or somatic. Until the existence and efficiency of DNA repair was known, it was reasonable to assume the linear dose-effect relationship prevailed, even down to minute amounts of radiation, but the persistence of that attitude is no longer acceptable. A much better case can be made for the opinion that background radiation is of no significance whatever and that at least 20 R must be surpassed before any residual effect that escapes repair is to be expected. On the linear-dose effect rule, not more than 1 percent of clinically significant mutations could be ascribed to background, and if, as I believe, much more rational ways of accounting for the 99 percent are available, then it seems equally rational to accept the 1 percent as also attributable to the rational cause. If we do this, we can, I think, replace the standard linear-dose effect graph (Figure 5-1a) by another (Figure 5-1b), in which a constant level is associated with error made during replication and the minor repair that is almost certainly a continual responsibility in every active nucleus. When external radiation creeps up to 100 R, with a greatly increased amount of repair being required, the incidence of error will of course rise proportionately. I want to defer most of the discussion of error proneness in DNA polymerase as the main factor concerned in mutation rate until we take up the subject of aging, in the next chapter, but it is logical for me to state here that it is the "rational alternative" with which I should like to replace the myth of the damage by minimal radiation doses.

In this preliminary discussion of mutation, it is desirable to mention some of the more general and evolutionary aspects of the process before going on to the medical aspects of somatic mutation in the next three chapters. The first is concerned with the evolution of DNA repair. According to my reading, the earliest particulate organisms, which were probably blue-green algae, were in existence 3000 million years ago, and since the earth took its form about 4500 million years ago, we can probably allow around 1000 million years for the first stages of evolution. During that period the "warm dilute soup" in the shallow seas of a lifeless earth slowly changed to give rise eventually to microorganisms, undoubtedly equipped with DNA and protein-synthetic mechanisms much like those of today's organisms. Oxygen was present in significant amounts only from some time in the Precambrian era, say 1000 million years ago; this means that throughout the 2000–3000 million years of evolution before that time there cannot have been any ozone in the upper layers of the atmosphere to check the ultraviolet from reaching the surface of the seas. One of the most important evolutionary requirements to be fulfilled over the course of those eons must have been to develop ways of counteracting ultraviolet damage to DNA. The les-

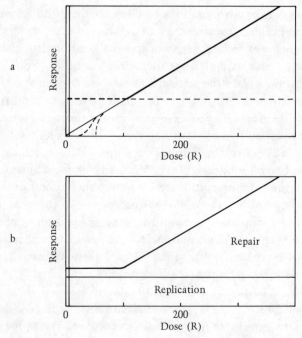

FIGURE 5–1. *A comparison of two ways of looking at the dose-response relationship to ionizing radiation. Part (a) shows the standard linear dose-effect relationship by which the response is taken as proportional to the dose over the whole range from zero upwards. The dotted horizontal line indicates the spontaneous incidence of mutants or malignancies. Any incidence below this will not be detectable as an effect of ionizing radiation, and the possibility of a threshold effect is indicated by the curved broken lines. Part (b) is based on the assumption that mutation results from informational error introduced into DNA in the processes of DNA replication and repair. In both parts of the figure, the vertical line at 7 R indicates the approximate amount of ionization received by human tissues in the course of a 70-year lifetime from "background radiation."*

son was well learned and all types of organisms have retained a basically uniform mechanism. Another difficulty in those first stages of evolution was probably a considerably higher background of ionizing radiation. The persisting radioactive elements, uranium, thorium, and potassium 40, all have half lives of about 10^9 years, and in the earliest days of DNA the background could have been six to eight times the present level.

Mutation is and must always have been the raw material of evolution. In the absence of mutation, change is impossible in the long term, but if mutation occurred at an excessive rate, too large a proportion of individuals would be nonviable, and unless some means of lowering the rate became available, the species would eventually become extinct. Somehow, evolution had to find a way by which a mutation rate appropriate to its purposes should be maintained. Modern work on the molecular evolution of proteins throws quite a new light on the frequency and importance of germ-line mutation. I find myself strongly in favor of Kimura's (1968) and Ohta's (1974) contention that most of the molecular changes in protein structure that arise during evolution are almost neutral in their effect on survival, and emerge mainly as a result of genetic drift. However, apart from noting their conclusion that a relatively constant rate of mutation may be maintained over long evolutionary periods, it is not appropriate to introduce that theme in the present context.

The first requirement for continuing evolution was to protect the newly evolved DNA from lethal damage by radiation, and the means developed was the mechanism of DNA repair that we have been talking about. Whether or not a repair mechanism completely free from the possibility of error is a biological possibility is of no significance. All that was needed was for the error rate to be reduced to something below the optimal level for evolutionary progress. Once that reduction was achieved, the way was open for a positive evolutionary control of mutation rates.

The functional efficiency of any enzyme depends first on the correctness of its chemical structure. This must hold just as much for the fidelity with which DNA polymerases achieve a precise replication of a DNA segment. Any degree of inefficiency, of error proneness, could be achieved by the same processes of germ-line mutation and recombination that have been responsible for the evolution of protein structure since life began. A well studied analogous situation can be found in the human glucose-6 phosphate dehydrogenase (G6PD), which is carried on the X chromosome. In the male, therefore, whatever allele is present is fully expressed. At least 80 mutants of the gene are known, and the degree of their pathological expression in males ranges from nil, through the well-known conditions in which a drug or a foodstuff is needed to induce an episode of hemolytic disease, to states of chronic hemolytic anemia for which no adjuvant is necessary. It is probably one of the many virtues of the chosen series of 20 biological amino acids that, by suitable point mutations, any degree of error proneness or of potentiality for a possible new function can be achieved and submitted to the test of selective survival. If there were good evolutionary reasons why a mouse should have a less efficient, more error-prone set of DNA polymerases than a man, Nature could readily arrange it. In the next chapter I shall discuss the evidence that she has done just that.

In this chapter I want to cover as many of the general aspects of mutation as possible, especially of somatic mutation, before we come to their more specific consequences for normal aging and for degenerative disease. At this stage it is appropriate to consider what are likely to be the observable results of mutational errors induced by the error-prone enzymes that we are beginning to postulate. The first point to be made is that, by hypothesis, the errors made will be rare and will affect at random any structural gene or any other functional DNA in the nucleus. The error could be in a gene, for one of the hemoglobin chains, for an enzyme such as G6PD, or for one of those still obscure gene-based functions that appear to control the organization of cells into multicellular structures. For each of these possibilities, the primary error is in the informational sequence of nucleotides, and the two immediate consequences are: (1) that the changed DNA will persist indefinitely in all subsequent descendants of the affected cell; (2) that the gene product will have a correspondingly changed amino acid sequence, and through a more or less complex chain of consequences give rise to what we can observe as the mutational effect.

From the practical perspective, when we are concerned with clinical appearances that suggest somatic mutation, the important task is to verify that a somatic mutation has in fact occurred. The standard difficulty is usually stated as that of distinguishing between a somewhat distorted process of differentiation, a subacute or chronic viral infection, and a somatic mutation. The decision may be very difficult and may often depend on definitions of what is or is not a virus or a mutation. The definition of somatic mutation I prefer is that of a change that occurs rarely and at random in a single cell and that is transmitted to all descendants of that cell. Implicit in the definition is the idea that the change is not equivalent to a normal step in differentiation, but the possibility is not excluded that error in DNA may result in a wrongly timed or otherwise abnormal "program," which in its normal form plays a part in differentiation. As long as the result is clearly abnormal and persists in clonal descendent cells, it is operationally a somatic mutation. The important consequence of such a definition, if (as is usual) we are concerned with a *population* of cells, is that there should be ways of demonstrating that the population is monoclonal if it has in fact arisen by somatic mutation.

In human material the standard approach is to use the enzyme G6PD (glucose-6 phosphate dehydrogenase) that I mentioned three paragraphs above in another context. In people of African origin, two alternative and easily differentiated forms of the enzyme A and B are both common. As a sex-linked condition, it is reasonably easy to find women who are heterozygous A/B, and for any common clinical condition (e.g., leukemia or uterine myomata) any considerable collection of African women patients will include some heterozygous A/B individuals. It is well established that all female somatic cells in mammals express the genes on one only of their two X chromosomes. It may be the paternal or maternal chromosome, but never both. What is particularly interesting is that the decision whether to express the paternal or maternal X chromosome is made at random early in embryonic life. In our heterozygotes for G6PD, about 50 percent of these embryonic cells express A, the others B. The descendants breed true, and the adult body therefore becomes a finely grained mosaic of A and B cells. A mutation affecting a single cell and producing, say, a benign tumor such as a myoma of the uterine wall will obviously be composed wholly of cells of the initiating cell's type, A or B, but never both. Similarly, if we have a condition that is either A or B but never both, we can say with almost complete certainty that it is a monoclonal condition and *must* have resulted from a somatic mutation. Difficulties in applying this criterion arise if the clonally multiplying cells are associated with inflammatory or other cells from various parts of the body. In general, proof of monoclonality is definitive proof of somatic mutational origin, but failure to demonstrate it does not always exclude the possibility.

The other general aspect that I should discuss in this chapter concerns the distribution and type of lesions that can arise when, for any reason, error affects in a somatic cell either a DNA polymerase or some other enzyme that is essential to the fidelity of any informational transfer between macromolecules. Transcription to mRNA is a process very similar to DNA replication and may use some of the same enzymes. Translation of mRNA to produce the primary polypeptide is a highly complex operation involving many types of enzyme. It is obvious that once errors creep into these processes, which are essential to every synthesis of protein in the cell, a self-accelerating process is liable to be initiated. L. E. Orgel (1963), who introduced this conception, believed that sooner or later such a process must end in what he called an "error catastrophe" and produce cell death. It is equally evident, however, that there will be infinite variations in the detail of such a progression of error into cell function, and corresponding differences in the intermediate stages and in the length of time elapsing before cell death. It is very probable that processes of this sort are basic to the widespread phenomena of cellular degneration that are associated with aging, and are probably the cause of it. My next chapter, which is on aging, will be, I hope, a logical sequence to this one.

AGING

ALL MEN DIE, AND THOSE who escape the hazards of youth and maturity begin at about sixty years of age to lose physical power and to grow more vulnerable to accidents of every description. The old man or woman develops the characteristic features of senescence, the gray hair, wrinkled skin, and diminished mental vigor. Each year the statistical expectation of life diminishes and death comes in one way or another between the ages of seventy and one hundred.

The inevitability of senescence and death has always provided a challenge to philosophers and scientists. I am very much aware of the appositeness of the remark that many biologists of past distinction have done no good to their scientific reputation by venturing on a theoretical interpretation of aging. No one has yet produced a satisfactory explanation of the whole process, and probably no one ever will. But much information has been gathered and every decade the understanding of the biological phenomena that are or may be relevant to the process has been improved. We can at least formulate the problems of aging more clearly, and I expect that we shall soon begin to see at least the outline of definitive answers.

We can look first at the evolutionary significance of aging and death. Death is more fundamental: it is something that can occur at any age and is not necessarily preceded by a period of senescence. Aging, however, always ends in death. Evolution is possible only when many more offspring are produced than will survive to reproduce in their turn. In no other way can we picture how mutations and new recombinations, most of which are potentially harmful, could be made to favor the changes toward greater effectiveness that we see as evolutionary progress. In nature, death without aging is the lot of most organisms. In fact one can say that modern man in an affluent society is the one living species for which this generality does not hold.

In some species there is no evidence of aging in the wild. For many small birds there is an exponential rate of death by predation. If for every generation of fledglings the mortality rate each year is 80 percent, less than 1 percent will be alive at the end of 3 years. If it were merely a matter of clearing the way for each new generation, there would be no evolutionary need for any process of senescence in such a species. The real evolutionary requirement for survival is that the individual should be adult and capable of reproduction within a single year: this will hold also for any other species subject to heavy predation or liable to catastrophic depopulation by flood or fire. If we examine the life patterns of mammals as being most relevant to our own, we can say that the greater the security of a life style, the smaller will be the average litter, the longer the time to reach reproductive maturity, and the greater the average lifespan in conditions of artificial security. It is as if the length of lifespan is an inevitable but evolutionarily unimportant manifestation of what was necessary to set the reproductive process to its proper tempo.

On such a view we need to look for some type of biological clock that, being set to give sexual maturity at time X, will ensure that average lifespan will be X^{1+y}. Unfortunately, biological timekeeping remains a mystery, and probably all that can be asked for is that any hypothesis of aging is not incompatible with this requirement. In brief, the effects of aging can be stated as:

1. a progressive decrease in the vigor and efficiency of virtually every measurable function, including muscular power, cardiac output, acuity of sensory perception, and so on;
2. probably associated with this decrease is the frequent evidence of atrophy and loss of cells from most, perhaps all, organs and tissues;
3. increasing vulnerability to trauma and infection;
4. increased liability to malfunction of the immune system, including autoimmune conditions, amyloidosis, myelomatosis, chronic lymphatic leukemia, and other lymphoid cell malignancies;
5. steadily increasing liability to malignant disease of almost all varieties.

Probably no one would quarrel with these statements. The problem is to identify a process by which such a condition, with effects on almost every cell in the body, could develop. The theories that have been suggested are:

1. wear and tear;
2. accumulation of genetic error (a) by somatic mutation, or (b) by withdrawal of genetic control;
3. progressive breakdown of the immune system plus secondary results arising therefrom.

Proponents of the wear-and-tear theory in its modern form cite the accumulaton of damaging effects by chemical substances that may be bacterial and other toxins from the gastrointestinal tract, or the effects resulting from oxidative processes affecting lipids in the cells generally. I shall not spend much time on this view, simply because it offers no approach to the aspects of aging that seem important to me. Wear and tear can be seen in the teeth of primitive people living on coarse natural diets, but the living cell and body tissues generally are essentially self-repairing units, and the idea of progressive wear and tear just does not make sense. There is no doubt whatever that chronic intrinsic or extrinsic poisoning can shorten life, but this cannot account for the characteristic features of aging.

The theory that aging is wholly or almost wholly the result of progressive inefficiency of the immune system is one that I was deeply interested in for many years, and it has been strongly advocated by Roy Walford (1969) and indirectly by Philip Burch (1968). I have no doubt that this progression is a very important factor in senescence and in initiating or allowing the final lethal episode, but I cannot consider it as primary. It is far more reasonable to look at it as one manifestation of a much more general and genetically based phenomenon. In one form or another we must consider the process as one of genetic error and try to formulate our theories in a form consistent with present-day thought in genetics and cell physiology. For obvious reasons our discussion will need to be based on the small number of mammalian species that have been adequately investigated in regard to the relevant parameters. Two species are outstanding in this respect: man and the laboratory mouse. Most of our discussion will center on those species, and the central problems are to determine, first, why there is an average lifespan of seventy years for men and two years for mice, and why certain characteristically age-associated diseases become prominent at the time of senescence in both species.

We can approach the first problem by looking over a series of domesticated mammals of known lifespan and recognizing that the character, average lifespan, is obviously genetically determined just as much as the size, hair color, or configuration of skeleton. In some way the requirement is coded in the genome and expressed in the processes, physiological and pathological, that are associated with aging. If we are to work within the experimentally accessible aspects of genetics, we are almost compelled to look for a set of structural genes that could be involved. From what I said in the preceding chapter, and from what I have written over the years, it will already be obvious that I regard somatic mutation as an extremely important part of the process of senescence. Indeed, the hypothesis of aging that I favor can be stated in three propositions:

1. average lifespan is determined by the rate at which somatic mutations accumulate in the body;
2. mutation results from error in the replication or repair of DNA;
3. degree of error-proneness depends on the structure of the enzymes concerned in repair and replication of DNA.

I shall try to develop the three points in sequence.

1. Somatic mutation as the basis of senescence. Aging is something that occurs in all tissues, and obviously produces secondary and tertiary effects of whatever may be the primary aspect of the process. The cumulative progressive character of aging is hard to explain on any other basis than somatic mutation. Once a mutation compatible with cell viability occurs, it persists indefinitely in the cell or its clonal descendants, and any further mutations persist similarly. I have for many years been impressed with Burch's stochastic mathematical approach to autoimmune and degenerative diseases, which centers on the nature of their age-specific incidence. In his view—and mine—the types of curve he obtains demand a basis of the general quality of somatic mutation. Differences of opinion may well arise on the specific cells in which the primary mutations accumulate, and I shall discuss this topic in my remarks on autoimmunity. Nevertheless, the curves that Burch obtains for such characteristic features of age as graying of the hair, fracture of the neck of the femur, and senile dementia seem to signify an accumulation of random changes whose result persists in descendent cells. Nothing but somatic mutation has the necessary qualities.

Much has been written about the Hayflick limit in relation to aging, and as I shall have occasion to mention it later, in connection with the diseases based on somatic genetic error, it must be considered here. Hayflick was primarily interested in using human cell culture lines for the cultivation of virus vaccines. This could have both advantages and possible dangers for that purpose. His cultures of fibroblasts were derived from the lungs of human fetuses of two to three months' development. Once established, stock cultures were preserved at liquid nitrogen temperature and used as seed for the production of working cultures. It was soon found, and has been fully confirmed since, that after cells had undergone transfers equivalent to about fifty cell generations, growth became irregular and soon ceased. If, as sometimes happened, it continued beyond this limit, the cells showed deviation from the normal diploid karyotype and had in fact become transformed toward malignancy. This rarely occurred, and such cultures are excluded from consideration.

Hayflick (1965) suggested that the fade-out at ± 50 cell generations might be the basis of aging, and perhaps largely because it represents one of the few available experimental approaches, the phenomenon has been extensively studied. There is a significant and progressive reduction in the level at which growth ceases as the age of the human donor of the cells increases. Mice have a limit of between 20 to 30 cell generations, as opposed to ± 50 in man. Robin Holliday, at the National Institute for Medical Research in London, has shown that cells in the terminal phase show a number of enzymes with abnormally low efficiency as judged by comparative immunological and enzymological assay (Holliday and Tarrant, 1972). This brings the Hayflick phenomenon into line with Orgel's hypothesis of aging (1963), devised by him to account for what may be happening in nonmultiplying (postmitotic) cells in the aging nervous system or other tissues. He was chiefly concerned about what would happen if error crept into the steps leading from DNA transcription to protein synthesis. Once this occurred, further errors could affect any enzyme in the cell, including those concerned in the fidelity of various transfers of macromolecular pattern. A process would be set in motion that would sooner or later lead to error catastrophe and death of the cell. This may well be one of the main ways by which accumulation of somatic mutations leads to progressive loss of cells, causing atrophy and diminishing efficiency of the organ concerned.

2. *Mutation from error in replication or repair of DNA.* Most of the relevant evidence for this second point has been given in the previous chapter. Here I am interested mainly in providing evidence that this mutation is directly relevant to the length of lifespan in different mammalian species. If our hypothesis is correct, the effectiveness of repair should be greater in long-lived than in short-lived species. Using a surprisingly simple experimental approach, Hart and Setlow (1974) have very clearly verified this correlation. Skin fibroblasts were established in cell culture from seven species of mammal, and standardized cultures were uniformly irradiated with ultraviolet. Tritiated thymidine was then added and the amount of "unscheduled synthesis" in 10 hours, a measure of the effectiveness of excision of dimers and repair of the gap, was estimated by autoradiography. Results showed that the amount of unscheduled synthesis was proportional to the ultraviolet exposure and progressively increased with the average lifespan of the donor species, as shown in Table 6-1.

TABLE 6-1. *Correlation of average lifespan in several mammalian species with efficiency of DNA repair in skin fibroblasts treated with ultraviolet irradiation.*

SPECIES	MEAN LIFESPAN (IN YEARS)	RELATIVE EFFECTIVENESS OF DNA REPAIR
Man	70	50
Elephant	60	47
Cow	30	43
Hamster	4	26
Rat	3	13
Mouse	2	9
Shrew	1	8

If one assumes that uniform ultraviolet irradiation produces the same incidence of thymine dimers in all nuclei, then the repair process in mice is very much slower and less complete than in the three large mammals. This is not a direct proof that the rate of mutation is higher in mice than in men. No evidence about mutation is given by this type of experiment. But there is evidence of ineffective repair, which would have a probable correlation with an increased number of ineffectively repaired nonviable cells as well as with an increased incidence of mutations. Similar relative inefficiency in replication of simpler types of DNA repair would have results of the same general quality with a probable dominance of mutational events over cell death.

3. The nature of error proneness.   An enzyme is a large protein molecule with a highly specialized structure; in a number of instances this structure has been determined completely, and in some an almost equally complete understanding of the catalytic action on the substrate has been provided. No such understanding has yet been possible for enzymes of such specialized function as those concerned with information transfer between macromolecules. However, one can be sure that they are at least equally complex and that their full function depends on their being of correct genetically determined structure.

Enzymes, like every other protein, can appear in mutant form. Many are known to exist in alternative forms, isozymes, each of which is apparently equally effective but distinguishable by electrophoretic or immunological procedures. In the previous chapter I spoke of the 80 known variants of the enzyme G6PD. In all probability, most or all of these variants could be regarded as error-prone mutants. Given the much simpler function of G6PD, one could hope that a chemical study of the variant enzymes might bring to light a pattern of error proneness or inefficiency that could help in the understanding of the infidelity of action that we are postulating for DNA polymerases or related enzymes.

It is easy enough to imagine how any appropriate degree of error proneness could be obtained by the replacement of amino acid residues by others. This of course is the standard process by which evolution proceeds. If the hypothesis of aging that I have presented is correct, it is not difficult, in principle, to provide a mechanism by which lifespan can be modified by evolution to fit a changing lifestyle.

Age-Associated Disease

The concept of old age in man includes, in addition to vulnerability to all types of damaging impacts of the environment, a whole series of what can be called age-associated diseases. Subject to minor qualification, one can define an age-associated disease as one which shows an age-specific incidence regularly increasing with age. The age-specific incidence is the number of deaths per annum experienced per 100,000 people in each five-year age group—0–4, 5–9, and so on. For many diseases the curve of age-specific incidence against age, when plotted logarithmically on both axes, yields, for the years from 40 onward, a straight line with a characteristic upward slope. For all cancers, it has a slope of 1 in 5, for enlarged prostate 1 in 11, and for senile dementia 1 in 17, and the line for each of these continues straight to the final age group of 80+. For other age-associated conditions the line curves downward at the highest ages. In general, this means that a genetically resistant group remains after almost all of those who are susceptible to the condition have succumbed.

Data on the age-specific incidence of disease in animals are naturally much less extensive than in man, but it is clear to all animal pathologists that what is found in animals examined when moribund with old age is broadly similar to the findings in senile humans. E. W. Goodpasture (1918), for instance, was struck by the almost universal presence of tumors, often multiple, in aged dogs coming to autopsy. Cardiovascular degeneration is usual; pigs show atheromatous lesions similar to those in the human. Atrophy and chemical changes in collagen parallel those seen in man. Qualitatively, the changes are all in clear correlation with a time scale based on average lifespan, not on years or decades.

Two aspects of aging and age-associated disease in mice should be mentioned.

90

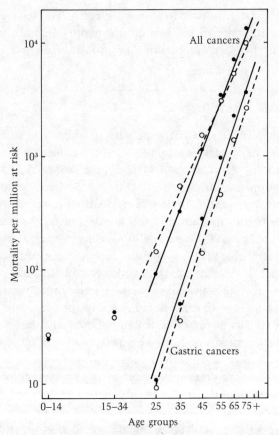

FIGURE 6–1. *The age-specific incidence of human cancer in males (solid curves) and females (broken curves). Two sets of curves, both plotted from Australian statistics, are shown: one for all cancers and the other for gastric cancers (of the stomach and duodenum). The mortality per million at risk is shown against ten-year age groups, both scales being logarithmic. From the age of 30 onwards all fall approximately on straight lines.*

1. A specific study of the incidence of malignant tumors in wild mice kept under sheltered conditions gave an age-specific incidence curve of the same slope as the human one, but the logarithmic age scale ran from 1 to 4 years instead of from 20 to 100. Our criterion for age association holds therefore for cancer in mice.

2. Studies on the effect of relatively heavy whole-body irradiation of mice with X or gamma rays show a shortened average lifespan, with an approximately parallel acceleration of malignant and other age-associated disease. There is also some increase in the incidence of malignant disease. Both effects are roughly proportional to the dosage of radiation. A point of some interest is that mice that have been given certainly lethal doses of X-irradiation and restored by infusion of normal bone marrow cells show larger numbers of tumors if they are allowed to survive indefinitely.

The foregoing data from animal experimentation are consistent with the hypothesis of aging and malignant disease as manifestations of somatic mutation, which in turn is related to error in DNA repair. Equally, in human clinical studies, all those age-associated diseases that are clinically important are more readily interpreted as resulting from somatic mutation than in any other way. As I have discussed in chapter 5, monoclonality is the best index of origin by somatic mutation. It means that the effective change was initiated in a single cell among many millions of similar cells that *might* have been similarly affected. It is a rare and random event, initiating a change that is transmissible to all clonal descendent cells. This categorically defines the essential process as somatic mutation, but it does not of course exclude the influence of other factors. There is not the slightest doubt that prolonged exposure to solar ultraviolet is an etiological factor in skin cancer, that heavy X-irradiation has produced leukemia, or that lung cancer is closely correlated with exposure to high concentrations of smoke from cigarettes. Also other less well known but equally significant evidence suggests that certainly for some and probably for all cancers genetic differences in susceptibility exist. I do not exclude the possibility that "slow virus" infection with persisting incorporation of virus DNA in the cell genome may play a part, although in man I know of only one established example, Burkitt's lymphoma. There is no doubt that evidence of Epstein-Barr virus (EBV) which is also an important factor in causing the disease infectious mononucleosis can be found in all cultures of Burkitt lymphoma cells, and the corresponding antibody in all patients' sera. But it is also a fact that *all* cultures of "normal" human lymphocytes show similar evidence of EBV, and the great majority of unaffected children in all parts of the world have EBV antibody. At least 80 percent of the lymphomas that have been tested are monoclonal, and the disease occurs only in children with persisting malarial infection. This is a good example of how complex the etiology of a human disease may be—and I shall be very surprised if there is not a genetic component still to be uncovered.

I think one can safely assume that every clinical condition that can be regarded as disease or abnormality involves:

1. individual genetic differences;
2. environmental impact involving infection, trauma, nutritional or toxic factors;
3. accidental circumstances of which the most significant is the occurrence of somatic mutation.

The relative importance of each group of factors in etiology must vary greatly from case to case, but all three are always to be seen. Secondary results are also usually present, and on occasion may be mistaken for primary ones. In human cancers the most important feature is somatic mutation, and most of my discussion of malignant disease in chapter 9 will be on this basis.

An entirely different type of clinical picture is to be seen in the effects of senescence, normal or accelerated, on cerebral and mental function in man. The neurons are cells that show no mitotic activity after early childhood, although they are metabolically intensely active. Their nuclear DNA does not replicate, but much of it is periodically active in transcription and there is evidence of a small regular amount of DNA-repair synthesis. From middle life onward there is a continuing disappearance of neurons from the cortex, cerebellum, and anterior horn cells of the spinal cord. In all probability this disappearance affects all sets of neurons and accelerates with age. For obvious reasons it is extremely difficult to give even approximate quantitative estimates of how this fallout of neurons proceeds. The commonly heard statement that every normal adult loses 10,000 nerve cells irretrievably every day of his life seems to be a mere guess. However, there is no doubt that the fallout accelerates with age and greatly so in senile dementia. At this stage the post mortem findings are atrophy of cortex and cerebellum, and great reduction in the number of nerve cells.

The interpretation must be rather speculative, but the most popular one is to regard the process as an example of Orgel's error catastrophe in action. Repeated unwinding, transcription, and rewinding of active segments of DNA must produce an occasional error and necessitate a call for repair, which in its turn will introduce a proportion of errors. Eventually error will occur in key enzymes concerned in transcription and the other stages of protein synthesis, initiating the cascading errors that give rise to a lethal error catastrophe and disappearance of the neuron. As in the clonal situation, DNA-repair errors will be a function of the error proneness of the key enzymes concerned. However, competitive selection for survival is absent in the postmitotic situation; the development of error catastrophe will be a very slow process, but like the number of errors it will accumulate with the years. Intuitively I feel that the rate of fallout of cells would closely parallel the curve of mortality with age.

Finally, in a brief discussion of the function of the immune system, I shall concentrate on the straightforward influence of its diminishing efficiency on protection against infectious disease. For many years I have cited the influence of age on death from respiratory infections during influenza epidemics to illustrate the overall changes of resistance with age. With great regularity one can plot the age-specific mortality shown logarithmically on the ordinates against age plotted logarithmically from 1 to 20 and linearly from 20 to 80+ in the abscissas to give two straight lines, coming to a minimum at the 10- to 14-year quinquennium (Figure 6-2). For reasons that have not been adequately analyzed, the 1918–1919 pandemic period showed a sharp difference from the mortality experience in "ordinary" epidemics before and since. Virtually everywhere the young adult mortality was conspicuous, usually more evident in men than in women. In mice the change is

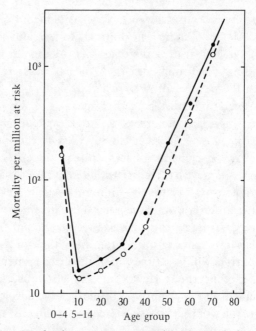

FIGURE 6–2. *Deaths from respiratory infections including influenza. The age-specific incidence for males (solid curve) and females (broken curve) shows a regular increase with age.*

fairly comparable, with a maximal level of antibody-producing potential at seven to nine months of age followed by a fall that accelerates with the onset of senescence.

Aging in both mice and men is accompanied by atrophy of the thymus, diminution of the circulating level of lymphocytes, and diminution of the peripheral lymphoid tissue. Subject to occasional discrepancies, the general rule is that capacity to give a secondary response when challenged with an antigen previously experienced remains high, but the individual fails to respond to a single dose of a "new" antigen. By repeated injection, however, it is often possible to build up an aged individual's response to normal levels.

The nature of vulnerability to infection in infancy is outside our area of interest and is probably affected by many factors that are not immunological. However, from the adolescent and young adult phase onwards, the phenomena are almost certainly primarily immunological. The peak of effectiveness in man is probably at about ages 20 to 25, but one must also take note of the fact that the severity of several types of first infection can be increased in adults by overactive immune response, particularly by T cells. From the young adult period onward the progressive diminution of the immune responses can be interpreted as due to an accumulation of mutational errors, leading by various routes to a diminution both in the number of extant clones and of the total lymphocytic population. At one time I felt that the evidence pointed to the probability that the Hayflick limit was of major influence in mediating this diminution in number and efficiency of immunocytes. Some relevant supporting evidence comes from Williamson and Askonas's experiments on transfer of pure clones of antibody-producing cells (1972), and their Hayflick-type explanation may be correct. However, on the basis of the interpretation I have given of the immune system as a whole, I suggest that it is an oversimplification.

Like any major biological topic, aging presents so many facets and impinges on so many adjacent fields of study that it is impossible — at least for me — to develop a theoretical treatment in a clear, consecutive linear fashion. One can only hope that from this interlocking discussion of immunity, senescence, and age-associated disease a tentatively satisfying picture will eventually emerge. At the present time I favor an interpretation of aging in the following form.

The accumulation of genetic error by somatic mutation is what allows the expression of average lifespan as the climax to the aging process. The *rate* of error and of somatic mutation in the significant cell types is what determines differences of lifespan between species or races of mammal. And this rate is an expression of the error proneness or inefficiency of the various DNA polymerases and other key enzymes concerned with DNA replication and repair. One must picture the normal individual of a species as having a coordinated level of error proneness in the key enzymes, which will allow a balanced increase in vulnerability. For good evolutionary reasons we must be prepared to find that coordination is based on some more subtle timekeeping processes concerned with reproduction, but we can provisionally think of it in terms of the aging process itself. The strongest evidence for the relationship between error-prone enzymes and average lifespan comes from the work of Hart and Setlow (1974) on ability to repair DNA damaged by ultraviolet.

To continue the same train of thought, a coordinated rate of error proneness of key enzymes throughout the cells of a given species would also be reflected in the rate at which *disease* initiated by somatic mutation would appear. This could include epithelial cancers, lymphoproliferative diseases like leukemia and myelomatosis, the CNS degenerative diseases, and atheroma, with its complications, and give them their age-associated quality.

In my eighth and ninth chapters I will elaborate this approach to the age-associated diseases, which for our species now provide the most important, or at least the most numerous, of medical problems. Before I deal with them, however, I want to discuss, in the next chapter, a group of rare diseases that appear to result from gross error proneness in DNA replication and repair. They provide an exaggerated, and therefore more readily comprehensible, picture of the processes that I believe are operating in aging and age-associated disease.

A NEW CATEGORY OF GENETIC DISEASE

Throughout most of the modern history of medical science, vital clues to the nature of normal function have been gained from the study of genetic disease. Three outstanding examples are diabetes, hemophilia, and sickle cell anemia. The last two are clear cut examples of Mendelian inheritance, indicating that the determining factor responsible for the clinical abnormality is carried by one or both alleles of a single gene. I should remind you that Mendelian inheritance may be autosomal dominant, autosomal recessive, or sex linked, when the gene is carried on the X chromosome, and just to recapitulate, the standard types of inheritance can be tabulated. The + and − signs indicate whether the characteristic abnormality is expressed by persons carrying all the alleles shown.

Autosomal dominant	AA $\times$ Aa $\rightarrow$ 2Aa + 2AA				50%
	$-$	$+$	$+$	$-$	
Autosomal recessive	Aa $\times$ Aa $\rightarrow$ AA	+ 2Aa	+ aa		25%
	$-$	$-$ $-$	$-$	$+$	
Sex-linked	Xx $\times$ XY $\rightarrow$ Xx, XX			$\female$	0%
	$-$	$-$ $-$			
	XY, xY			$\male$	50%
	$-$ $+$				

As the chart shows, when an individual expressing an autosomal dominant gene (a heterozygote) mates with a normal person, 50 percent of the offspring are normal and 50 percent are heterozygotes showing symptoms. Autosomal recessive genes are expressed only symptomatically in 25 percent of the offspring of heterozygotes. The parents of an individual expressing a recessive trait are always heterozygous carriers. In sex-linked diseases the mother is always the carrier, and any males with the anomalous x gene express the disease.

It must be remembered, however, that many alleles produce no clinical signs although their existence can be recognized biochemically or immunologically, and others can show any grade of intermediate action. In chapter 6, I mentioned G6PD genes as an example in which such a grading can be seen.

DNA polymerases and the other enzymes concerned with DNA replication and repair introduce a different dimension. Looked at simply as enzymes, they behave as any other enzyme. If structural change from the normal is excessive, the enzyme will be completely inert and no repair or replication will take place. Less extreme change will produce an inefficiency of function that can be measured by standard enzymological methods appropriately modified to the circumstances. The commonest approach is to expose a suitable cell culture to standard doses of ultraviolet or ionizing radiation and follow the process of DNA repair by a suitable method. Incorporation of labeled nucleotides may be incomplete or unduly slow, or breakage of DNA strands may fail to be mended, as judged by centrifugation experiments. The new dimension emerges when we find that, in addition to such standard changes, the presence of the mutant allele is also associated with abnormally frequent somatic mutational change.

For various reasons the most commonly studied form of mutation is "point mutation," involving a single nucleotide change in a structural gene with a corresponding amino acid change in the gene product. However, the likelihood that most of the lesions observed as a result of somatic mutation may be due to mutation in "control DNA" has been suggested in chapter 5 and will be expanded in the final chapter. Both types should be kept in mind, since a similar change in nucleotide sequence will differ greatly in its observable effect according to whether the DNA concerned is part of a structural gene or has a control function. It will be simpler and more enlightening, however, when we are thinking about DNA polymerases or any other enzymes, if we concentrate on what happens in structural genes and their gene products.

The first point to be stressed repeatedly is that the DNA of any normally proliferating mutant cell must be fully functional; it is not damaged DNA, but since the mutant quality persists indefinitely in descendent cells, it is informationally modified DNA. The qualitative change of nucleotide is not a direct or inevitable result of the changed structure of the DNA polymerase; it is one of the accidents that have become more likely because of the inefficiency of the enzyme. The enzyme is unduly error prone, but the precise mechanism responsible for each nucleotide replacement may have to remain unanalyzed. My reading would suggest that in particularly favorable material it might be possible to correlate the deviation of the enzyme from the "wild" form with both its efficiency of repair and the type and distribution of informational changes induced. For the present we can take only a stochastic approach to the informational changes and assume that their overall rate of appearance, irrespective of type, is a function of the error proneness of the enzyme. In chapter 5 I have described how it has been shown in two examples from a virus and a bacterium that modification of a DNA polymerase can increase the mutation rate at all the loci tested.

In this chapter I am concerned with what happens when germ-line mutation results in an unacceptably high degree of error prone-ness in DNA polymerase or in one of the enzymes concerned with DNA replication and repair. The classical prototype of such condi-tions has emerged in the last few years as the disease xeroderma pigmentosum (X.P.). The characteristic skin lesions that give the disease its name are limited to exposed areas of skin and are ob-viously caused by the action of the solar ultraviolet component on skin epithelium and melanocytes. If, as I believe, the disease results from delayed and error-prone repair of DNA damaged by ultra-violet rays, it is advisable to recapitulate here an outline of the process of damage and repair. The primary damage is a fusion of two adjacent pyrimidine bases, usually two thymines, with the produc-tion of a thymine dimer, which, while it exists, prevents replica-tion of the DNA strand involved. Unless it can be repaired, the lesion renders the cell nonviable. Repair is a complex process com-prising enzymic recognition of the presence of the dimer, its exci-sion by combined endonuclease and exonuclease action, and reconstitution of the segment by methods that differ according to the extent of the damage. The result is usually the full reconstitu-tion of all damaged DNA, the liability to mutational error being greater if postreplication repair is necessary than if simple single-strand repair is required.

Ultraviolet damage and repair, as I indicated in chapter 5, was the first type of reversible change in DNA to be studied, and in all probability one of the first great evolutionary developments was the perfecting of the repair process. It was natural enough, therefore, that the possibility of X. P. representing some inadequacy of DNA repair should stimulate the first experimental approach into the field we are interested in.

Xeroderma pigmentosum is a rare genetic disease afflicting not more than one newborn infant in 250,000; it is inherited in Mendelian fashion as a typical autosomal recessive condition, i.e., only one gene is primarily responsible for producing the syndrome. Because of the lesions elsewhere than in the skin that are found in

X. P., it is important to keep the Mendelian quality of its inheritance constantly in mind.

In describing a typical case of xeroderma pigmentosum, let us begin with the skin lesions. The skin is normal at birth, and usually no abnormality is noted until the child is exposed to outdoor sunlight for the first time. It then becomes obvious, from its redness and blisters, that the skin is highly sensitive to light. Intense freckling appears by two years of age and continues on all exposed areas through life. The published photographs indicate that the freckles have the same general character and diversity of size and deepness of pigmentation that is seen on the face of a thin-skinned Celtic small boy. Personally, I have no doubt whatever that all types of freckles derive from somatic mutations in which ultraviolet and DNA repair play a part—and some of the strongest evidence for that statement comes from xeroderma pigmentosum. Not even dermatologists seem to be particularly interested in freckles, and it is the next stage in X. P. that is of central clinical concern. At about the age of eight or ten the first skin malignancy appears, usually a basal cell carcinoma, common enough in outdoor workers in their 60's and 70's but never in normal children. In the old days, more tumors developed and most patients died before they were 20 years old. Under constant surgical surveillance the early tumors can be satisfactorily treated, and several patients have had more than 100 histologically certified tumors removed.

A point I find very impressive is that when the tumors are distributed according to type, the order of frequency is: (1) basal cell carcinoma, (2) squamous cell carcinoma, (3) acanthoepithelioma, (4) malignant melanoma, (5) rarer tumors, including hemangioma, sarcoma, fibroma. This is precisely the order of skin tumors found in elderly men who have lived much of their lives outdoors in tropical or semitropical climates such as that of Queensland in the north of Australia. After making an attempt to estimate the relative exposure to ultraviolet of these two populations, taking into account both average intensity and duration of exposure and bearing in mind that X. P. patients will avoid direct sunlight as much as possible, I believe one can say with reasonable confidence that X. P. patients suffer from the same types of skin cancer and in the same relative proportion as normal people, but at a rate not less than 10,000 times the normal. That could be a very important statement when it comes to discussing the etiology of cancer.

Experimental studies have naturally been centered on cells derived from the skin. It is a standard technique to initiate cell cultures from a small biopsy of human skin, the cells taking on the standard fibroblast form as they develop in the culture. The reported experiments all compare the behavior of such cultures from X. P. with those from a normal person. Routinely, a well established culture is given a standard ultraviolet exposure, tritiated thymidine is added, and the uptake, indicating so-called unscheduled synthesis, is measured by autoradiography. At the National Institutes of Health (NIH), in a continuing study of 13 patients, 12 showed varying degrees of delay in thymidine uptake, but when representative examples were followed for 30 hours, all reached the control level of uptake (Robbins et al., 1974). By complementation studies it appeared that several genetic units could be influencing the delay in repair, but it should be noted that all the cases showed quite closely comparable skin lesions of X. P.

In the very recent literature one finds accounts of studies using other methods of checking the physiological efficiency of repair of ultraviolet damage to DNA. As a result, several patients with X. P., in whom DNA-repair appears to be normal by one criterion but abnormal by another, have been described. Taken with the complementation studies, this seems to indicate a complex situation in which a number of different types of inefficiency or error proneness within the complex of DNA-repair enzymes can each give rise to informational errors of similar type. The mutational changes indicating informational change in DNA cannot be studied in cell cultures, but there is no reasonable alternative to ascribing them to error arising in the process of repair. The essential genetic defect therefore must be ascribed to the gene coding for whatever enzyme in the repair complex is responsible by its error proneness for the informational anomaly.

The story of the skin lesions in X. P. is thus for the time being clear enough; but there is more to X. P. than that. Five of the 13 cases in the NIH series suffered from congenital abnormalities of the central nervous system. This has been well known for many years, and cases showing particularly well marked nervous symptoms have been given the separate name of de Sanctis-Caccione syndrome. A variety of neurological signs and symptoms may be found, of which the most often noted are microcephaly with mental retardation, absence of tendon reflexes, and athetotic movements and other cerebellar signs. In an investigation of two patients with absent reflexes, myographic records and muscle histology indicated that a continuing process of motor neuron loss was going on.

All these signs are too rare in medical experience for there to be any question of coincidence; the central nervous system (CNS) lesions are as much part of the genetic anomaly as the skin freckles and cancers. The only conclusion I can draw is that the faulty gene also codes for DNA replication and repair concerned with developmental processes in utero which can have no relationship to ultraviolet irradiation. At this stage the most important deduction from this is that we now have justification for looking at genetic conditions with similar CNS lesions but no X. P. as also possible results of error-prone DNA-handling enzymes. It is worth pointing out that findings on the nervous system give a further indication of the complexity of the structure of DNA polymerases and of the existence of different complexes in different organs and tissues.

Rightly or wrongly, I regard this work on X. P. as providing the most important conceptual advance in medicine since 1950. The potential pathogenicity of error-prone DNA repair and replication enzymes is clearly established, the somatic mutation theory of cancer is conclusively confirmed and a reasonable source of those mutations identified, and a new approach to a wide range of genetic conditions with multiple manifestations in different tissues is shown. Finally, it greatly strengthens the probability that the intrinsic mutagenesis hypothesis of aging is correct. What was originally a typical armchair hypothesis has now a strong clinical and experimental background of support.

In *Intrinsic Mutagenesis* (1974) I included two chapters on diseases that from clinical description seemed to be possible candidates for inclusion as conditions based on an aberrant gene coding for an error-prone DNA repair or replication enzyme. One of these, Fanconi's anemia (pancytopenia), has recently been shown to be inefficient in DNA repair. A third group of diseases of the skin that should be studied for the presence of error-prone repair enzymes has since been added.

Information was sought in catalogues and atlases of human genetic diseases, and particularly in the standard catalogue of human genetic conditions showing Mendelian inheritance by McKusick (1971). In working through such a catalogue, one cannot avoid being impressed by the complex symptomatology of many of the conditions described. Some are undoubtedly the result of secondary or tertiary effects of a single biochemical abnormality. Many others may have a basically similar but still unrecognized primary cause.

Using X. P. as a prototype, I have attempted to detect Mendelian conditions in which focal lesions are conspicuous, in order to see whether an interpretation in terms of error-prone DNA polymerases is possible or likely.

Discrete focal lesions that are clearly associated with a Mendelian genetic process may have any one of several alternative origins.

1. The lesions may result from some environmental stimulus, parasitic or chemical, which is lesion-producing only on the appropriate genetic background. I cannot recall any examples.

2. The genetic background abnormality in every cell greatly increases the likelihood of a visible somatic mutation. The example of retinoblastoma in Knudson's interpretation can be taken as a prototype. Indirect evidence is impressive, but there is still no visible methodology for detecting the genetic quality of the predisposing abnormality. Some of this predisposition could be the result of an error-prone DNA polymerase, but various other causes could be imagined.

3. The error-prone DNA polymerase hypothesis has the outstanding advantage that in most instances it will be susceptible to experimental support by the detection of a biochemical deficiency in DNA repair. It must, however, remain very much a possibility that a DNA polymerase complex is not detectably deficient in DNA repair but has a significantly increased probability of inducing informational error. One example of X. P. was found in such a category.

It is a not unreasonable postulate that any anomaly of DNA structure that is physically possible will sooner or later occur and that error-prone DNA polymerases will increase the probability of its occurrence. As our acquaintance with the wilder shores of genetic theory gradually increases, it becomes possible to enumerate the various ways in which informational error could become manifested as somatic mutation in the broad sense. First, we can take the ways in which a nucleotide segment may be altered:

A. point mutation, including base replacement and frame-shift mutation;
B. anomalies involving a significant length of polynucleotide strand: deletion, inversion, somatic intragenomic crossover;
C. abnormalities at chromosomal or chromatidal level.

In A and B the change can affect (i) a structural gene with corresponding anomaly in the gene product, usually inefficiency or loss of a certain enzyme function in all cells; (ii) structural genes concerned with enzymes responsible for fidelity of macromolecular synthesis; and (iii) repetitive genes (control DNA; operators) in which the change expressed is in a genetic program, not as a structural modification of enzyme or other gene product. Morphological aberrations in chromosomes must for the time being be simply indicators that changes at the level of DNA have also occurred and that some fairly gross failure of complete repair has ensued.

With this background we can look at a number of "candidate diseases" that might have an etiology analogous to that of X. P.

1. Neurofibromatosis and other skin diseases. Multiple neurofibromatosis is by far the most important candidate for consideration. It is an autosomal dominant condition of reasonably common occurrence; the rate for new mutations, approximately 1 per 10^4 births, is the highest for any human genetic disease. It is also, to my knowledge, the only human genetic condition also sometimes seen in a form thought by competent geneticists to be a primary somatic mutation.

The clinical features of multiple neurofibromatosis are pigmented "café au lait" spots and scattered neurofibromatous tumors in the skin or arising from subcutaneous nerves. Skeletal anomalies and bone cysts will be found in most adult patients, and mild degrees of mental retardation are unduly frequent. Most patients would be classified as of low normal intelligence or moronic, a defect presumably related to the same genetic process. It seems highly probable that the main cells affected, melanocytes and Schwann cells, are derivatives of the neural crest, but this leaves the skeletal lesions and possible cortical effects unexplained. There is no evidence that ultraviolet radiation in any way causes the pigmented spots; in fact "freckles" in axilla and the perineal area are said to be diagnostic. In most subjects the neurofibromas appear first in the second decade, and develop to varying degrees. At least two authors (Nicholls, 1969; Crowe et al., 1956) have described cases in which skin involvement is limited to one segmental area which may have five or six neurofibromas with none elsewhere on the body. Crowe has not wholly convincing evidence that such cases are of somatic mutational origin and are not inheritable.

This is a brief outline of a condition that fulfils all the criteria I laid down, but to date there is no experimental evidence at all, either for or against the hypothesis. One would assume that the enzyme at fault is characteristic of neural crest cells and that mutation in the controlling gene is common at the germ-line level. However, an important alternative approach has been proposed by Nicholls. It is essentially the assumption that the neurofibromatous lesions are composed of, or initiated by, cells homozygous for a gene N, the lesion being the specific expression of the NN condition.

The individual is born as a heterozygote N+ with no lesions; these appear only when a somatic mutation converts + to N to give the homozygous NN condition. S. Ohno (1974) has suggested, in a different context, that the appearance of a homozygous NN cell could also arise in replicating cells by a process of somatic crossing over and subsequent nondisjunction. There is probably no way by which this process could be differentiated experimentally from other types of somatic mutation. It would in fact be a somatic mutation, according to the definition I have used, and it is at least an interesting thought that the rare abnormal process needed to produce NN from a heterozygous cell might be associated with error-prone enzymes. The difficulties of Nicholls' interpretation are that NN homozygotes at the germinal level are unknown— the possibility that NN is lethal at an early stage of development should be studied—and it is necessary to ascribe the café au lait spots and the bony lesions to the same gene. The apparently dominant quality of multiple neurofibromatosis inheritance offers no difficulty if there is a regular appearance by somatic mutation of typical lesions in all heterozygotes. It is clear that the interpretation of multiple neurofibromatosis will have to await experimental study of the repair and replication enzymes, but for the present I would consider it better to work on the alternative N+—NN interpretation. The key feature, however, is still a somatic mutation.

Several other skin conditions follow this general pattern with discrete skin lesions of reasonably uniform character developing at various times through life, usually with some other lesions apparently of developmental nature. All of them are very rare, and the only one I shall say anything about is the nevoid basal cell carcinoma syndrome. These lesions are scattered over the skin, but appear mostly on the face, neck, and shoulders. They arise from basal epidermal cells and produce small tumors, usually of very low malignancy. When lesions form in palmar or plantar epithelium, they are finally extruded, leaving characteristic long-lasting pits. In addition to the skin lesions, numerous and very disparate lesions appear elsewhere; jaw cysts and skeletal anomalies of various types, endocrine disturbances such as sexual underdevelopment and parathormone unresponsiveness, and medullablastoma brain tumors have all been reported. Inheritance, as in the others of these skin conditions, is autosomal dominant. A point of interest is that although there may be as many as 1000 lesions on a single individual, the great majority of the tumors are nonmalignant. A small proportion, however, become typical malignant basal cell carcinomas, so providing strong evidence for the contentions that malignancy results from somatic mutation and that more than one mutational step is usually necessary for the full development of malignancy.

In other analogous conditions the focal lesions are warty keratoses, sebaceous adenomas, small smooth-muscle myomas, cystic epitheliomas, and self-healing keratoacanthomata. All are inherited as autosomal dominants and all present the same sorts of difficulty of interpretation as multiple neurofibromatosis. A special feature of this whole group is that in each subtype there is a characteristically uniform type of focal lesion not seen in xeroderma pigmentosum. This has implications that are not covered by the hypothesis of a straightforward error-prone DNA polymerase etiology. If each focus is the manifestation of error affecting only a small porportion of cells, then the errors are not occurring at random but are limited to an essentially identical region in each affected somatic genome. A more probable alternative is that the distribution of the lesions is due to the dispersion of intermediate descendent cells that are derived from a specific somatic mutation in an early stem cell. Monoclonality studies would probably decide the proper interpretation.

2. *Genetic conditions that are manifested in multiple tissues.* This group of diseases is rather a mixed bag of conditions that have two or more of the following characteristics: (1) genetic condition with proved or probable Mendelian inheritance; (2) lesions of diverse type and location; (3) evidence of chromosomal abnormality on karyotyping; (4) evidence of anomalous behavior in DNA replication and repair; (5) undue prevalence of malignant disease; (6) signs of premature aging.

In *Intrinsic Mutagenesis* I included three fairly well known but still rare conditions in a first subgroup. These are Fanconi's anemia, Bloom's syndrome, and ataxia telangiectasia, each with either four or five of the "markers" I have named. All three show breakage and atypical forms of chromosomes in cultures, both of lymphocytes and of skin fibroblasts. Very recently, Fanconi's anemia fibroblasts have shown delay and incompleteness of repair of ultraviolet damage. There are no reports on the other two. People afflicted with Fanconi's and Bloom's conditions are prone to leukemia; ataxia telangiectasia shows a variety of neoplasms, mostly lymphoreticular, and is also said to show signs of premature aging. My impression, derived wholly from reading, as I have never seen a case in the flesh, is that all three, and some other more obscure conditions, may be variants of a single condition arising from various types of inefficiency and error proneness in a single DNA-handling mechanism.

The regularity of chromosomal abnormalities in these conditions would make one postulate that the single gene whose abnormality gives rise to the syndrome must code for an enzyme whose normal activity is necessary if chromosomal integrity is to be maintained as well as for efficient DNA repair and replication. Two important points are raised by that conclusion: (1) that the physical disruption or rearrangement of a chromosome may be responsible for the way mutations are expressed; (2) that it may be possible to use karyotypic changes to indicate the probability that DNA repair and replication enzymes are not functioning efficiently.

The second subgroup comprises progeria and Werner's syndrome, the classical examples of accelerated aging. Progeria is extremely rare, and the claim that it is an autosomal recessive condition is not fully substantiated although it is plausible enough. Pictures of Gifford's original case have appeared in most textbooks since: a 10-year-old child appearing like "a frail little old man" with a nearly bald head fringed with thin white hair, and a small beak-nosed face. A particularly interesting feature is that the patients die between 15 and 30, virtually always from conditions based on widespread atherosclerosis, such as coronary heart disease, cerebral hemorrhage, or aneurysm. If one considers this in relation to the

Benditts' finding (1973) that the primary atheromatous plaques are monoclonal accumulations resulting from somatic mutation, the feeling of the significance of somatic mutational error for aging is strengthened. Werner's syndrome is a less extreme type of premature aging: a reasonably normal infancy and childhood is followed by failure of the adolescent growth spurt, graying of the hair at 20, and then other signs of senescence, including cataract, with death usually in the 40's. Atherosclerosis is seen in all subjects, and diabetes in about 50 percent; cancer in 10 percent is of much earlier onset than in normal people.

Cultured fibroblasts from the skin of subjects with either progeria or Werner's syndrome are difficult to work with. It is claimed that both have a greatly reduced Hayflick limit and that incomplete enzymes are found in early cultures. The DNA repair capacity is a subject of controversy, but one is disposed to believe the report showing that the time required to mend X-ray breaks is much greater than that required for mending breaks in normal cells.

In the absence of clear evidence of Mendelian inheritance, both conditions could well be interpreted as resulting from more than one set of homozygous defects coming together in the affected individual.

3. Degenerative disease of the central nervous system.   The third group contains a number of degenerative age-associated diseases of the central nervous system. In the first place we have, perhaps in a continuous series, the minor mental disabilities of healthy old age, senile dementia, which is said to be an autosomal dominant with 40 percent penetrance at the age of 90, and Alzheimer's disease, in which signs of senile dementia come on at an abnormally early age. If the interpretation I gave of mutational error in postmitotic cells leading to what Orgel (1963) calls "error catastrophe" is correct, this condition is an example of a normal aging process pushed to a pathological intensity but manifesting no clear point at which normality can be separated from disease.

A discussion of more specific degenerative diseases—Huntington's chorea, Friedrich's ataxia, motor neurone disease, and the complex degenerative disease, amyotrophic lateral sclerosis/ Parkinson dementia, found in an exceptionally high proportion of the Chamorro people of Guam—will be found in *Intrinsic Mutagenesis*. It is at present, and likely to remain, an armchair speculation that these are also manifestations of error-prone repair and replication enzymes. Experimental studies on DNA repair of several types are practicable with lymphocytes or skin fibroblasts, but it seems unlikely that any equivalent way of handling human neurons will ever be devised. So I shall do no more than mention the probability that some relationship between the group of degenerations of the central nervous system and our general concept will eventually be found.

I might summarize this chapter as an attempt to demonstrate the importance and complexity of somatic genetics in relation to human disease and how the hypothesis by which I have tried to provide a link between the evolutionary need for an appropriate average lifespan and the expression of senescence in cumulative somatic error can perhaps be turned to the understanding of certain varieties of genetic disease. I have also said a good deal about conditions in which malignant disease becomes a very conspicuous part of the picture of error accumulation. In the next two chapters, on autoimmune disease and cancer, I shall elaborate on the somatic mutational approach to malignant disease, giving an implicit picture of autoimmune disease as a form of conditioned malignancy.

AUTOIMMUNE DISEASE

I STARTED MY MEDICAL career in 1923 and I have been able to watch a whole series of fashions in diagnosis and in interpretation of human disease come and go. Some conditions are clear-cut: by the 1920s most of the important infections were well defined, but a majority of the illnesses that brought people to an outpatient department were of unknown origin. They could often be given a name and for some there were traditional methods of treatment that seemed to be effective. Rheumatoid arthritis, hemolytic anemia, Graves' disease, diverticulitis, and pleurisy can be taken as representative of the more definite syndromes. But in addition there were and are innumerable cases of localized pain—headaches, sciatica, fibrositis, skin rashes, disturbances of alimentary function, hysteria, depression, and anxiety. At various periods there were distinct fashions in the way these obscure conditions were looked at. They might be disorders of the ductless glands or result from septic foci—a favorite diagnosis in the 1920s that led to wholesale removals of teeth, tonsils, and appendixes. There are still many diseases of unknown etiology, and fashions still have their sway. Today the popular fashions are to diagnose illnesses we don't understand as autoimmune conditions or slow virus infections.

Autoimmune diseases are interpreted as conditions in which the necessary normal taboo on immunological action against cells or other normal components of the body has broken down. Cells are being damaged by antibodies or by specifically aggressive lymphocytes, or the kidney glomeruli are being blocked by autoantigen-antibody complexes. In most of these conditions autoantibodies can be detected in the blood, but then to make things more difficult, a small proportion of apparently healthy people also have autoantibodies in their blood and the proportion increases with age. Examples of conditions in which autoimmune phenomena are conspicuous include rheumatoid arthritis, pernicious anemia, thyroid disease, diabetes, and systemic lupus erythematosus (SLE). There is no unanimity of theoretical approach to autoimmune disease, but all workers will probably agree that the first approach to understanding must be to define the modifications of the normal immune reactions that are involved in each example under study.

In my summing up of the functional organization of the immune system in chapter 4, I made the point that it could be regarded as a homeostatic and self-monitoring system of mobile cells so structured that there was a high possibility of meaningful contact between any two cells of the system. In addition, informationally significant molecules are being released into body fluids by immunocytes under conditions many of which have been defined. The known substances of this nature are the immunoglobulin antibodies and lymphokines. There is strong evidence for the existence of a third group of unknown chemical structure, transfer factor. It is known that lymphocytes are dependent for proper functioning on an appropriate concentration of insulin and cortisol in the plasma, and there may be other requirements not yet defined, such as a thymic hormone.

All these interactions are mediated by genetically controlled receptor proteins on lymphocyte cell surface, antigenic and effector molecules also on the surface, and by equally specific and genetically controlled macromolecules in solution. It is evident that for the optimal functioning of such a system, the large number of complementary macromolecular patterns involved must be of correct genetically defined types. It is equally essential, however, that "fail-safe" methods must be available that enable somatic mutational or other types of change in a cell or a cell line to be neutralized before the whole system is endangered. Everything points to the immune system having a unique flexibility that allows it to react, usually effectively, to the infections and other relevant emergencies that may arise. Sometimes, of course, the flexibility is overstretched and immunodeficiency or any one of a wide range of immunopathological conditions may develop, often with a lethal issue.

It is in line with modern thought on immunology to use this model of the immune system in discussing the nature of autoimmune conditions. It will be necessary, however, to point out the experimentally accessible aspects of the system that seem to be of special importance in connection with autoimmunity.

1. Almost by definition any autoimmune situation requires the functional presence of a specific receptor reactive with an accessible self component. This may be the combining site of an antibody or of an immunoglobulin cell receptor, and if, as I have assumed, there is a non-immunoglobulin receptor present on T cells, and even possibly on B cells, that too must be a possible candidate to become self-reactive. At one stage I was inclined to take it as self-evident that autoimmune reactivities not found in normal individuals must signify the presence of abnormal cells. Since everything pointed to the clonal origin of these cells, I could see no reasonable source of this abnormality other than somatic mutation. This is probably still an important factor, but modern work on the significance for immunological tolerance of B and T cells makes it reasonably certain that there are normally circulating B cells with receptors that are potentially reactive with self components but that are kept clinically inert for other reasons to be mentioned later.

2. It is clear that, when specific contact of an effector with an immunocyte produces a signal, the results can vary, depending on a number of factors; in general, there may be positive stimulation leading to surface activation, mitosis, proliferation, and synthesis of specific antibody or lymphokine; hyperstimulation, with death or sterile differentiation; and negative or inhibitory effects. In Figure 4-1 I have tried to express a tentative generalization about how positive and destructive responses are related to certain parameters. The pattern shown is speculative, but it is consistent enough with the facts to make me fairly confident that an important factor in autoimmunity is an increased resistance to being inhibited or destroyed by antigenic contact. There is evidence from the New Zealand Black (NZB) mice that this is a germ-line quality, and from studies of the HL-A antigens in man, that there is an important genetic component in some human autoimmune diseases.

3. There is good experimental evidence that when competent immunocytes are transferred to an irradiated host they will not proliferate unless specific antigen is also provided. It should follow that cells which, for reasons 1 or 2 above, are potentially capable of autoimmune proliferation will not do so if the amount of antigen accessible in the body is insufficient. It may be necessary that the target organ be infected, traumatized, or otherwise altered before the antigen becomes accessible in adequate amount to stimulate the potentially dangerous cells into pathogenic clones.

4. In chapter 4 I said something about immune surveillance against malignant cells in the context of the self-monitoring function of the immune system. Surveillance is more effective against malignant lymphoid cells than against any other type, a point that I shall elaborate in the next chapter. Most autoimmune diseases are subject to some degree of regression, and occasionally complete remission occurs. It is immaterial whether one ascribes this to immune surveillance or to the activity of suppressor T cells; whatever the mechanism, it probably represents the most important of the "fail-safe" provisions.

5. If a lymphocytic cell line is proliferating out of the normal homeostatic control and as a result producing bodily damage, it conforms to the standard notion of malignancy. It is really irrelevant that in the case of an active autoimmune disease we know (or assume) that proliferation of the pathogenic clones depends on their stimulation by an accessible autoantigen. It can reasonably enough be called a conditioned malignancy but it is still a malignant condition. The more one learns about lymphocytic pathology, the more one is impressed with the continuity of autoimmune conditions with more overtly malignant processes, especially chronic lymphatic leukemia, Waldenström's macroglobulinemia, and multiple myelomatosis. It is significant that autoimmune hemolytic or thrombocytopenic disease is a common terminal complication of chronic lymphatic leukemia and that a significant proportion of the myelomas and macroglobulinemias have monoclonal globulins that are autoantibodies.

6. Much remains to be learned about the immunological implications and overtones of the processes by which effete and damaged cells, the debris from healing areas of infection or trauma, and antigen-antibody complexes are dealt with in the body. Where the point has been specifically studied, there is no more than a transient appearance of autoantibody without symptoms, if there is anything at all. The process by which red cells are systematically removed by splenic macrophages after around 100 days in the circulation would obviously repay closer study from an immunological perspective. Surely some as yet unrecognized fail-safe mechanism must be at work here. I would not however accept the contention that all autoimmune disease is based on deviations of these processes that clean up outdated cells or tissue debris.

7. Finally, one must mention the possible role of aging and of pathologically intense error proneness in DNA polymerases and associated enzymes in immunocyte lines. In the chapter on aging, I indicated how close I am to Walford's contention that aging is or may be mediated wholly by immunological processes. Even if, as I believe, the immune system is only one of the cell groups subject to the processes that cause senescence, it may well be the most important. The immunological features of old age include a group that can be labeled immunodeficiencies, inability to react to new antigens, disappearance of T-cell-mediated reactions, susceptibility to death from infections that would be negligible in maturity. A second group of immunopathological conditions, presumably associated with more specific results of cumulative somatic mutation, contains several autoimmune conditions, notably rheumatoid and other chronic arthritides, as well as an increased incidence of autoantibodies. Chronic lymphatic leukemia and the monoclonal gammopathies are characteristically age-associated diseases of the immune system. Hodgkin's disease will probably be identified as a viral disease analogous to EBV and Burkitt's lymphoma, but particularly in the age-associated form of lymphosarcoma of Hodgkin's type it may have major qualities of nonviral neoplasia of an immunocyte line. It is noteworthy that nearly all the conditions I have mentioned under immunopathology in old age—rheumatoid arthritis, the gammopathies, and Hodgkin's disease—are associated with amyloid deposition. Most pathologists probably regard amyloid as the debris left from essentially autoimmune interactions of immunocytes and antibody with body components.

With those seven sets of relevant factors as a background, one can analyze with some confidence the problems presented by autoimmune disease and the appearance of autoantibodies without symptoms as they are encountered in clinical work.

First, some general points may be mentioned. It is highly characteristic of autoimmune disease to be multiform in its symptomatology and its course. Most cases develop insidiously, and in any normal population a few individuals will show one or more of the standard autoantibodies without symptoms. Diagnosis is frequently difficult and it seems likely that each individual patient must be studied, not so much to determine which of the conventional diagnoses seem to be most nearly appropriate, but to assess the type of process taking place in the individual. Rheumatoid arthritis in several named forms, Sjögren's disease, and systemic lupus erythematosus merge into one another. Even when a definite single diagnosis, say rheumatoid arthritis, can be given with certainty, the distribution of affected joints, intensity of local inflammation and of general symptoms, and range of positive laboratory tests will vary greatly from case to case. This of course is just what would be expected if the disease resulted from an accumulation of one or more aberrant clones of immunocyte operating under partial control in a very complex system.

Another aspect of some general significance is the age incidence of onset of the commoner or more clearly definable autoimmune diseases. In some conditions, such as rheumatoid arthritis, it is more convenient to follow the proportions of people at various age segments who show evidence of disease. Burch (1968) has studied pertinent data intensively, and has constructed stochastic equations to fit the patterns obtained. In his view a very large proportion of subacute and chronic diseases, including some generally accepted autoimmune diseases, give specific age incidence curves that are consistent with a process by which random changes occur uniformly over the period from birth onward. Once they have occurred they leave a persisting change in the afflicted cell and in its descendants. Somatic mutation is the only biological process of the required quality, but the analysis does not define in what cell line the mutational events occur. Burch assumes that all degenerative disease, including aging, is due to the impact of autoaggressive cells on various cells and tissues. Maynard Smith (1962) and others are doubtful of the justification for Burch's detailed analysis into the relative parts played by germ-line abnormality and by cumulative somatic mutation in a single line or in multiple lines of autoaggressive cells. All I believe worth emphasizing about Burch's work is that the general pattern points to the importance of rare and random processes occurring at a definable rate over a prolonged period of time. In other words, they do not in any way controvert the hypothesis of accumulating somatic mutation.

It is of interest too that the incidence of autoantibodies increases fairly regularly with age, and work in Australia has given an intriguing indication that in an old person the presence of autoantibody is to some extent a presage of early death.

Autoimmune Hemolytic Anemia (AHA)

Let us now consider the main groups of autoimmune disease, beginning with autoimmune hemolytic anemias. These are usually, and I think correctly, regarded as resulting directly from the damaging effect of the easily demonstrable autoantibody in the circulating blood. The symptomatic and immunological diversity of the classical "warm" autoimmune hemolytic anemia is immense. Unlike most autoimmune diseases, it can affect any age, from infancy onward. Some, particularly those of infancy and those secondary to infections, recover spontaneously; others are acutely fatal, most are long lasting and subacute. The autoantibodies are usually detected by a positive Coombs test; the patient's red cells are apparently unaffected but carry a coating of incomplete antibody that is detected by testing the cells with a rabbit antiserum against human immunoglobulin. Agglutination of the cells represents a positive direct Coombs test. In other cases the autoantibodies can agglutinate or hemolyze the patient's own cells directly. Study of the specificity of the autoantibody usually shows it to be directed against one of the minor Rh antigens, c or e in the Fisher terminology, but sometimes no such specificity is demonstrable. The suggestion that the condition results from any one of a large number of essentially random mutational episodes is inescapable.

Two other types of autoimmune hemolytic anemia that I shall mention only briefly are the "cold" type AHA, and paroxysmal hemoglobinuria, or Donath-Landsteiner disease. The cold AHA occurs mainly in older people and resembles a monoclonal gammopathy. The autoantibody attaches to red cells only at 20°C or lower, and is present in large amount in the circulating plasma. Donath-Landsteiner is also due to a cold antibody which, when the blood passes through cold hands and feet in winter, causes in vivo hemolysis and the appearance of hemoglobin in the urine. In the great majority of the cases of all three diseases that have been tested a monoclonal antibody is present. The presence of this antibody is an indication to me that the situation is primarily related to a mutational change in an individual B cell, but I am equally certain that other factors are necessary—probably germ-line genetic in most subjects, but in some it is clear that the use of a drug, notably α-methyl dopa, has been a contributing factor. In Donath-Landsteiner disease, congenital syphilis appears to have been associated with the syndrome.

Further analysis of AHA makes it necessary to look at the position in the only well studied animal model of the disease, the New Zealand Black (NZB) mouse. These mice develop a typical enough warm type AHA at about six to eight months of age, with a positive Coombs test. They have a number of other immunological abnormalities, including positive reactions against some component of cell nuclei, the so-called ANF reaction, and they usually die from antigen-antibody complex nephritis. Young animals have an abnormally active response to most antigens and usually fail to be rendered tolerant by standard manipulations. Later in life there is evidence of abnormality in T cell suppressor function.

The important points in the interpretation of the NZB condition seem to be:

1. The immunological characteristics are inherited in autosomal dominant fashion, two genes being involved according to N. L. Warner (1973).

2. Although in NZB the antibody is polyclonal, it is monoclonal in Fl hybrids with C57B1.

3. Cells capable of producing autoantibody are present in small numbers in the spleen before the antibody is demonstrable in the blood. The numbers increase greatly with the onset of serological changes.

4. Transfer of the condition to young NZB mice is possible only with spleen cells, the implication being that both antibody-producing cells and the effective immunogen are concentrated there.

5. Lymphoreticular malignancies are common in later life and may be related to the loss of suppressor T cells or other immunological factors.

6. Different authors have isolated four different viruses from NZB strains and each has suggested that his virus is responsible for some aspect of NZB pathology. I remain skeptical.

My current and perhaps unduly simplified interpretation of NZB is that the strain is genetically a "super responder," presumably because of a genetic abnormality. An autoantibody is, after all, the product of an unduly active producer cell that is not as active as it should be to tolerization. On such a germ-line background, quite minor somatic mutation could give an initiating cell that would overcome normal controls, whether these are in the form of suppressor T cells or something else.

There is very much more to be said about human and murine AHA, but I think the essence of autoimmunity has been described in this section.

Systemic Lupus Erythematosus (SLE)

The only other autoimmune disease that I should like to say something about is systemic lupus erythematosus, always abbreviated to SLE. This is the autoimmune disease *par excellence*—at least as much in the variability of its intensity and the range of tissues affected as in the unique character of the associated autoantibodies. Clinically, SLE is commonest in young women and has a wide range of possible symptoms—facial rash, painful joints, pleurisy, albuminuria. The diagnosis is usually made only when lupus erythematosus cells are demonstrated to appear in blood held outside the body. I won't go into the fairly complex technique of the test; it is enough to say that a positive result is due to one or more of the autoantibodies against nuclear components of circulating leucocytes. Many different autoantibodies may be present, but the best studied are those that react with DNA and with a variety of DNA fragments and other materials that can be released from actively multiplying and damaged cells. SLE can often be fatal, and death is nearly always a result of kidney failure, which arises essentially from blocking of the glomerular filter by antigen-antibody complexes.

No one is sure what causes SLE, but many guesses have been made. Some look for a virus or a sensitizing protein from the bowel. Others, myself included, consider it as a genetic and somatic genetic disturbance, giving an unstable immune system that may be triggered into dangerous self-accelerating activity by some trivial infection or emotional stress. It is an interesting exercise to see whether one can interpret the immunological phenomena accompanying SLE in terms of the modern view of the immune system that I have tried to depict. My interpretation may turn out to be quite wrong, but perhaps the attempt will be enlightening even if the solution is a false one.

In discussing tolerance I emphasized that T cells seem to be more important than B. For probably all the potential antigens to be found in the body, B and T cooperation is necessary for antibody production, and if no appropriate T cells are present, B cells whose receptors and potential antibody have specificity for an autoantigen will fail to respond to such antigens. If, however, we postulate the appearance of a clone of T cells which, irrespective of what passive Ig receptor they are equipped with, show enhanced resistance to what would normally be tolerizing contact with specific antigen, we can devise a rather interesting scenario that might even be close to the truth about SLE. By hypothesis, any cells of the clone appropriately armed with the necessary IgM receptors will react with some lymphocyte surface antigen by proliferation and release of mitogenic lymphokine and will not be tolerized or inhibited by high concentrations of the specific autoantigen. Let us assume that our potentially pathogenic cell must find itself in a site at which lymphocytes are proliferating, say, a germinal center in a lymph node. Very rapidly a clone of descendent, autoreactive T cells begins to build up and mitogenic lymphokines are liberated. Any B cells of appropriate reactivity, and especially any that are reasonably resistant to inhibition by excess antigen, will be set into proliferative and synthetic activity. This will include *all B cells reactive to any of the products liberated by multiplying and necrotic cells.* It is characteristic of all regions in which there is active lymphoid cell proliferation to find pyknotic nuclei and other evidence of cell damage and necrosis. In a situation in which one set of lymphocytes is reacting against other sets and being stimulated to proliferate as a result, the process will be an auto-accelerating one and it will spread to other areas of lymphoid tissue, notably the thymus. In a severe case of SLE one has the sense that a civil war is making chaos of the immune system. All sorts of autoantibodies and autoantigens are in circulation and the normal homeostasis has gone. Soon the accumulation of antigen-antibody complexes in the kidneys and other sites, such as joint linings, leads to serious illness and death.

The scenario has many possible variations, especially if the pathogenic autoimmune clone is less resistant to control than the one we had chosen, or when skilled use is made of corticosteroids in therapy. In all probability germ-line factors are concerned in SLE, perhaps such as those we have postulated for NZB mice—a certain general vigor of immune response and resistance to tolerizing.

Other types of autoimmune disease—rheumatoid arthritis, pernicious anemia, thyroid disease, and so on—could be treated in similar fashion. Each has its own individualities, and in most it is necessary to allow for the interaction of other factors than those that are wholly intrinsic to the pathogenic immunocytes. In particular, extraneous triggering factors may determine the time at which symptoms are initiated, and one must always consider the need for a continuing source of accessible autoantigen to drive the process once it has been initiated. What I am more interested in for purposes of this discussion is a fairly new genetic approach to autoimmune disease.

I have already mentioned the set of major histocompatibility antigens possessed by every species of vertebrate. Typical examples are the H2 antigens in mice and HL-A in man. In both species two genetic loci are responsible for major histocompatibility antigens so that the HL-A type in most individuals is comprised of four units: on rare occasions both alleles at one or the other locus may be identical. Details of the methods by which the HL-A formulas for large numbers of people can be obtained are irrelevant. All that need be said is that reagents and techniques are now sufficiently standardized for comparable results to be obtained in different laboratories, and since about 1973 great volumes of such data have poured into the literature. Some investigators have been specifically interested in the racial distribution of the types, but as I have indicated earlier, much more research has been concentrated on a search for correlations between susceptibility to disease and particular types.

The most striking of these relationships concerns ankylosing spondylitis, a not particularly rare disease in which 90 percent of the subjects have antigen W27 as one component of their histocompatibility type. In control populations about 7 percent have W27. Before going further, it is necessary to point out that presence of a W27 antigen does not foredoom a person to ankylosing spondylitis. Calculations indicate that only 1 or 2 percent of persons with W27 develop spondylitis, but that is about 140 times the probability in persons without the antigen. It is clear that no direct causal relationship exists between antigen and the initiation of ankylosing spondylitis. It is evident, however, that the gene for W27 is quite closely linked with another gene that alone or in some polygenic combination is responsible for susceptibility to the disease. This does not of course eliminate the possibility that an infective or toxic agent from the environment is a cause, but if no such environmental agent can be recognized, as in ankylosing spondylitis, the correlation with an HL-A antigen is an a priori justification for assuming that genetic factors are important.

McDevitt and Bodmer (1974) have published a table of the results of HL-A tests they regard as significant. I have shortened it by eliminating conditions in which the correlation of a certain group with a disease, although significant, showed only a small increase in susceptibility as compared with the general incidence of the disease (Table 8-1). In my shortened list we find the following conditions: (1) ankylosing spondylitis, Reiter's disease, acute anterior uveitis; (2) psoriasis; (3) Graves' disease, gluten-sensitive enteropathy,

TABLE 8-1. *Autoimmune diseases showing correlation with HL-A group*

NORMAL INCIDENCE IN POPULATION	DISEASE	INCIDENCE OF GROUP IN PATIENTS WITH DISEASE
W27 (7%)	Ankylosing spondylitis	90%
	Reiter's disease	76%
	Acute anterior uveitis	55%
HL-A8 (23%)	Graves' disease	47%
	Celiac disease (GSE)	78%
	Dermatitis herpetiformis	62%
	Myasthenia gravis	52%
	Chronic hepatitis	68%
W15 (8%)	Systemic lupus erythematosus	33%

Source: After H. O. McDevitt and W. F. Bodmer, "HL-A, immune-response genes, and disease," *Lancet* 1, 1269–1275 (1974).

celiac disease, dermatitis herpetiformis, myasthenia gravis, chronic hepatitis.

You will have noticed that there are only two sorts of disease in this combined list—diseases commonly regarded as autoimmune plus one example in which a common environmental antigen produces a pathological degree of sensitization. The implication seems to be clear that HL-A-linked specific immune response genes in mutant form may predispose the subject to autoimmune disease or pathologically overactive sensitization to certain foreign antigens.

You will also have noticed that the antigen HL-A8 was the one most frequently associated with five different diseases: four autoimmune, and one sensitization. This antigen is important in a different connection that may also be highly relevant to medicine. When the distribution of HL-A antigens in large numbers of normal people is examined, it is found that the combination of HL-A1 at the first locus and HL-A8 at the second locus on the same chromosome is very much more frequent than would occur with random distribution. This is what is called "linkage disequilibrium," giving undue frequency to the haplotype HL-A1, HL-A8. As would be expected, the 1, 8 condition holds for most of the five diseases with HL-A8 association. Any disequilibrium of this sort should arise only when there is, or was in past generations, some significant advantage for survival of any subpopulation having that particular combination of genes. Given the crowded and insanitary character of urban living throughout most of European and Asian history, that advantage could most probably be ascribed to resistance against death from infections during childhood. Any inheritable quality that provides increased resistance to the commonest conditions that are lethal before reproductive age is reached is bound to spread through the population. In the event that the haplotype 1, 8 combination had such an effect, it necessarily follows that in the absence of conditions for which the disequilibrium is of survival value, continuing recombination will inevitably bring the antigens back toward a random association as haplotypes. The linkage disequilibrium will slowly revert to the normal equilibrium, and any special quality associated with it will disappear. In other words, the average resistance of children to potentially lethal infections will diminish.

It is possible that we are beginning to see this shift already. As a consequence of the greatly increased interest in immune deficiency disease, large numbers of hospital patients, particularly any who seem unduly prone to infection, have been examined immunologically. Quite substantial numbers have been found to have recognizable anomalies, such as deficiencies in one or more of the immunoglobulins. In addition, it is well known that many children are more susceptible to the ordinary infections of childhood than others, but do not manifest any significant immunological abnormality. Most of the differences in resistance to infection probably have a genetic background whose relation to immune response gene action is indicated by the linkage with certain HL-A types. Until extensive HL-A typing of these unduly susceptible groups and of healthy individuals has been completed and analyzed, this suspicion, that genetic deterioration of this sort is taking place, must remain a mere speculation.

A phrase I once used in regard to autoimmune disease was "forbidden clone." It has persisted, though nowadays it is usually mentioned only when someone wants to decry the idea. Here I should like to set out my ideas on that point as clearly as I can. Where an autoantibody is directly responsible for the disease, and especially if it is monoclonal, as in hemolytic anemias, thrombocytopenia, and perhaps Graves' disease, I believe one must postulate an inherited mutational change in the clone, which renders some normal surveillance process inactive. The resulting pathogenic clone may then rightly be referred to as a forbidden clone, even though other genetic or drug factors may also be necessary if the forbidden clone is to flourish. Here we are dealing only with a B cell and its descendants.

In most forms of autoimmune disease we can be reasonably certain that antibody as such is not pathogenic. Here I believe that we must keep the following points clearly in mind: (1) B cells can be programmed to produce an autoantibody, but in the absence of helper T cells they will never do so; (2) T cells with a passively accepted IgT receptor of autoantibody pattern will normally be eliminated by contact with the antigen, but can by germ-line and/or somatic mutation become resistant to that elimination; (3) accessibility of the autoantigen in the body is important if pathological effects are to develop.

All types of study show that when tolerance is tested and recognized by failure of antibody production, a T cell population is tolerized (i.e., inactivated or destroyed) more rapidly and with a smaller concentration of antigen than a corresponding B cell population. Nevertheless, B cells can be rendered tolerant by appropriate doses of antigen.

In summary, then, autoimmune disease can be regarded as evidence of a partial breakdown of the homeostatic and self-monitoring quality of the immune system. On any current theory of how immune pattern is produced, B cells, bearing receptors and liberating antibody, both of them with combining sites reactive with self-components, must be constantly produced. No doubt a proportion with high affinity for accessible autoantigens will be destroyed or tolerized, but many will persist, and in the absence of other necessary factors will have no pathogenic effect.

The interpretation of T cells as being activated or armed with monomeric IgM receptors received passively from B cells is as applicable to autoimmune phenomena as it is to the normal immunological responses discussed in chapter 3, but it is still not accepted by more than a minority. I can see no escape from assuming that the main etiological factor in autoimmune disease is a somatic mutational change to what can be called a resistance to tolerization in one or a limited number of T or B clones. These clones, therefore, can still legitimately be spoken of as forbidden clones. Part of that resistance may also be developed by germ-line mutation or recombination. In addition a number of fail-safe mechanisms of still unclarified nature are almost certainly present. As these mechanisms progressively break down with age or for other reasons, conditions may allow the appearance of autoimmune manifestations.

Although some conditions seem to indicate an undue vigor of certain clones, most autoimmune phenomena are manifestations of a tendency to immune deficiency. What is required for normality is the balanced functioning of our homeostatic and self-monitoring system. Autoimmune conditions are basically an indication of disbalance—often at more than one point—in the immune system.

CANCER

IN CHAPTER SIX I discussed cancer as an age-associated disease and implied that somatic mutation was the essential step in its origin. However, an equally strong view prevails, particularly in the United States, that although it may be semantically legitimate to speak of somatic mutation as the immediate process leading to cancer, the practical task is to find the environmental factors, physical and chemical carcinogens, and cancer viruses that are responsible. In most respects I agree with that approach as being thoroughly in line with the whole tradition of preventive medicine. Epidemiological studies of the incidence of cancer have been conducted according to age, sex, occupation, and race, and some according to country, social and cultural customs, evidence of inheritance, or clustering of cases; indeed, this sort of investigation has probably been the most important source of clinically important knowledge about the origins of human cancer.

In this chapter, however, I want to balance the practical with the theoretical, and concentrate on three of the aspects of neoplasia that have interested me in recent years: genetic and somatic genetic aspects, the significance of environmental factors, and immunological surveillance.

Findings Bearing on Genetic and Somatic Genetic Origin of Cancer

1. Retinoblastoma is a malignant disease of the eye seen in infants. It can appear only during the period before retinal cells mature, and though the condition is usually fatal if untreated, enucleation of the afflicted eye or eyes is often curative. At least a proportion of such treated cases, when they become adult, have children with retinoblastoma, and it is possible for a sibling of a case to be unaffected but to have an affected child. Knudson (Knudson et al., 1973) has analyzed statistics of retinoblastoma and finds that he can cover the facts completely on the following assumptions:

a. All retinoblastomas depend on a sequence of two gene anomalies.

b. The second anomaly is always a result of somatic mutation in the patient.

c. The first anomaly may be of germ-line origin or it may occur as a somatic mutation. The first group (germinal + somatic) usually show more than one tumor, the second group (somatic + somatic) never show more than one.

d. What are necessarily rough calculations indicate that the frequency per relevant cell of the primary germinal and the primary somatic mutations are of the same order.

Similar but not quite so clear-cut results indicate that two other human tumors, neuroblastoma and pheochromocytoma, have a similar origin. I can see no conceivable way by which a virus or an environmental carcinogen can have any effect on these conditions.

2. In discussing xeroderma pigmentosum, I emphasized that solar ultraviolet was undoubtedly a contributing factor in the appearance of the skin cancers—that the different types of these cancers showed the same relative frequency as in normal people exposed to much greater amounts of ultraviolet. I estimated that the number of malignant tumors that would be produced by the same total exposure to ultraviolet in xeroderma pigmentosum patients would be at least 10,000 times the number obtained in normal persons. The significant action expressed by the double recessive gene, which I have claimed to be the error proneness of an enzyme concerned with DNA repair, could, rather loosely, be said to be 10,000 times as important as ultraviolet in causing the cancers. Again, it would take some very special pleading or self-deception to attribute any part in the process to a virus.

3. In xeroderma pigmentosum, various types of mole (lentigo) —nonmalignant but some very similar to and eventually giving rise to malignant melanoma—are common. So also are keratoses, which on section are not readily distinguishable from early epitheliomas. Everything suggests the presence of premalignant clones of mutant cells and implies that overt malignancy is attained by sequential mutation.

4. A more precise indication of this is given by two rare genetic conditions of the skin, characterized by multiple small tumors. They are almost certainly to be interpreted as resulting from a recessive germ-line gene which can be expressed only when a second somatic mutation involving the normal allele takes place. The situation is very similar to that of the inheritable type of retino-blastoma.

One is the congenital nevoid basal cell carcinoma in which the small tumors have the histology of basal cell carcinoma but are virtually never malignant in the clinical sense. When they occur in palmar or plantar skin they are eventually extruded, leaving characteristic and permanent pits. The second is apparently limited to descendants of a single mutation, which occurred in the west of Scotland some time before 1790. This is the self-healing squamous epithelioma most often seen on the face that may develop to a centimeter in diameter and then regress (perhaps by an immunological process), leaving a deep scar. In both conditions we seem to have stabilized mutant clones of epithelial cells on the verge of malignancy, but never becoming overtly cancerous.

5. In discussing chromosomal changes in cancer, German (1974) finds that the great majority of human cancers show some form of chromosomal abnormality on close examination. Often only one chromosome is altered, but the abnormality is visible in all cells of the cancer, thus indicating their clonal character. With one exception—the Ph chromosome in chronic myelocytic leukemia—there is no specific anomaly characteristic of a given type of malignancy. The new chromosomal appearance is unique to the patient and the neoplastic process concerned. Similar findings have been noted in experimental cancer, in which it is possible to follow a fairly regular development of further chromosomal abnormalities as the tumor develops and is passed to new hosts. No one has seriously suggested that the chromosomal abnormalities are causally related to cancer. The simplest interpretation is that, whenever somatic mutations occur, there is a substantial likelihood that the affected cells will show an altered karyotype that is transmitted clonally if any proliferative advantage goes with the mutation.

A fairly comprehensive study of work by German and others indicates that it is probably legitimate to use karyotypic change from the individual's norm as an a priori sign of somatic mutation. This not only brings most or all cancers into the class of somatic mutations, but suggests that both the malignant change and the karyotypic anomaly are secondary to error in DNA repair or replication. Most or all of the classical physical or chemical mutagens that have been adequately studied can be shown to produce karyotypic changes. Since in most laboratories karyotyping is likely to be more readily available than capacity to measure DNA repair rates, and because a single cell in metaphase can give the information, it provides an important means of handling the experimental and observational material in this general field.

Repetitive DNA

In this book I have so far neglected one very important aspect of modern genetics: the presence and possible significance of repetitive DNA in all mammalian and other eukaryotic cells. I believe that opinion is still unformed about the interpretation of this large amount of DNA in short segments (± 300 nucleotides), which is for the most part present in the form of tandem interpolations between structural genes. In view of the clear need for elaborate control of the timing of gene activation or repression, plus the dogma that all information in a cell is carried by DNA, the hypothesis is virtually inescapable that in some way repetitive DNA is responsible for this control function and that one should distinguish between structural DNA and control DNA.

Work in this area is very active at present, and my knowledge of it is far behind the growing edge of discovery. However, I should like to refer to two papers from Milstein's laboratory in Cambridge: Milstein et al. (1974) and Proudfoot and Brownlee (1974). They epitomize the modern position better than anything else I have found, and have the added advantage that they are primarily concerned with immunological material, namely, messenger RNA for the light chain of a mouse myeloma protein. This mRNA contains approximately 1250 nucleotides of which only 642 (321 + 321) correspond to the V and C domains. The rest is made up of untranslated material and a sequence of 200 poly-A units. The poly-A is added after transcription but all the rest is presumably derived from the DNA sequence, corresponding to control DNA. Functions for it are suggested by Milstein's group as translational control, termination of transcription, the addition of poly-A, and messenger RNA degradation.

What is even more interesting is that the corresponding 5' UT (untranslated) section for *globin* mRNA is very closely homologous

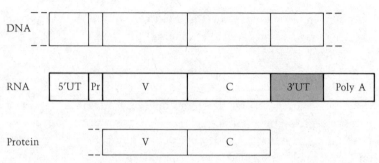

FIGURE 9–1.   *The relationship of untranslated DNA to structural DNA.
The corresponding segments of DNA, messenger RNA, and protein are
shown for light chain of a mouse immunoglobulin.* [*Data from Milstein
et al., 1974.*]

in structure to that for immunoglobulin light chain, and presumably
performs the same functions and is perhaps similarly related to the
translated sequences of all mammalian structural genes. This
concept provides a much clearer idea of the function of repetitive
untranslated DNA. Though it is yet to be demonstrated experimentally, one can feel certain that other untranslated sequences
of DNA are concerned with the switches from one program to
another that are constantly required, particularly in embryonic
development, but equally so in every process of the development of
functional cells from persisting stem cells during adult life—even
the switch from IgM to IgG can be taken as a simple example.

Untranslated control DNA must be subject to the same types of
damage and to errors during repair and replication similar to those
affecting the region responsible for the structure of the gene
product. Although there can only be speculations about the way by
which error in control genes is expressed, most of the complex
abnormalities of cellular behavior appearing as somatic mutations
must arise from genetic error in control DNA with or without
associated structural gene mutations.

It is in relation to malignant change that the need to invoke
mutation in control DNA is most evident. Attention was drawn to

its importance largely because of the frequent, perhaps universal presence of fetal antigens in malignant cells, antigens not present in normal adult cells, which presumably arise by an "erroneous" activation of genes that have been latent since their close down during or soon after the fetal period. One of the more attractive of the "biological" interpretations of the characteristics of malignant cells is that one or more of the mutational events needed for overt malignancy is a mistimed and otherwise abnormal activation of a "program" that should function normally only at some earlier stage of development. There are many possible examples, the most interesting being the suggestion made long ago that the very first differentiation in the placental mammalian embryo, the formation of trophoblastic cells, might be an important prototype of cancer. You will remember that the trophoblastic cells for a period invade the uterine mucosa in cancerous fashion to allow the implantation of the embryo. There are many other occasions in development or in adult life when active proliferation or other cancerlike activities of normal cells are initiated for longer or shorter periods. Since it is a dogma of genetics that every somatic cell contains the full content of information in the zygote, including all the programs of coordinated gene activations and repressions, we can in principle assume that any one of those programs can be called into activity by random error. Even a superficial consideration of the process of cellular differentiation and morphogenesis will indicate the extremely large number of program changes taking place during the variable periods of active proliferation that must occur in every cell line. In the absence of firm, experimentally based knowledge it is reasonable to assume that the switch-off of such programs will be dependent on the achievement of some interim developmental goal and the receipt of an appropriate feedback "message" from adjacent cells that have reached that goal. Any program activated in error in later life will only rarely find any effectively equivalent feedback and will need to be inhibited by some makeshift fail-safe expedient, one of which might be immune surveillance, against the now operatively alien "fetal antigens" that are likely to be present. An interpretation of this sort is better than any alternative for explaining the extreme heterogeneity of cancer's histological type, invasiveness, and susceptibility to local control. Malignancy, according to this view, is not a unitary disease; it is the result of any inappropriate activation, through somatic mutational error, of a proliferative program that remains uninhibited and uncontrolled by any morphogenetic, immunological, or inflammatory processes that can be brought into action against it.

Undoubtedly, when more is known about control DNA, rules on the likelihood with which various programs are reactivated by mutational error will emerge. Whether it will ever be possible to go beyond broad general statements is more than doubtful. The more I learn about the fine structure of the mammalian cell and the complexities of intracellular and intercellular interactions and controls, the more I am convinced that detailed understanding of the malignant process and practical control of cancer based on understanding will never be possible. The most we can hope for is to develop an adequate knowledge of what effects intrusion of environmental factors into the system may induce, and some notion of the relationship between frequency of cancer and the intensity of the intrusion.

The Action of Environmental Agents in Cancer

In a discussion of the cancer problem published in 1957, I committed myself to a mutational theory of cancer, regarding environmental factors as "essentially" providing conditions that increased the frequency of mutation, and being very much inclined to believe that cancer viruses were a laboratory artifact of little or no significance for human malignant disease. My attitude really hasn't changed very much since that time. There is still no established evidence that any human cancer can be regarded as basically due to a viral infection. This holds even for Burkitt lymphoma, in which all tumor cells give evidence of EB virus.

What I want to discuss is how the approach to somatic mutation that I have adopted bears on the very important problem of environmentally influenced cancer. Two environmental factors are fully established as important in the causation of common human cancers: exposure to solar radiation and skin cancer; cigarette smoking and lung carcinoma. The evidence that certain types of skin cancer are more frequent in workers exposed to tar, soot, or lubricating oils, and bladder cancer in persons working with naphthylamines, and that bone sarcoma used to occur in a high proportion of dial painters using radium salts, is equally unequivocal. It seems highly probable too that environmental factors we can expect to be defined quite clearly in the next decade contribute to cancers of the colon, in which lack of roughage in the diet seems to initiate a complex process leading to cancer, and cancers of the cervix uteri, where early and frequent intercourse can initiate a similar process. In both these examples the evidence is essentially epidemiological and the immediate carcinogen, if it exists, is not yet identified.

The approach to understanding skin cancer from solar radiation has been provided by the studies of xeroderma pigmentosum that I described in the preceding chapter. The presence of a wide variety of premalignant epithelial and pigmentary lesions suggests that a cumulative mutational process is necessary for overt malignancy, but there is no reason to seek for any other process at each step than the sequence of dimer excision and error in repair of DNA that has been described in earlier chapters.

Economy of hypothesis is achieved if a basically similar process is assumed for the other examples of environmental cancer: i.e., that an environmental agent entering the cell produces, in a certain proportion of instances, damage to DNA that can be repaired, but with a correspondingly increased chance of informational error. The nature of each mutational change in the genome is always random, but the occurrence of premalignant proliferative change following one mutation, making movement toward malignancy more likely on subsequent mutations, may be important.

In cigarette cancer of the lung, the entry of carcinogenic hydrocarbons into cell nuclei and the resultant production of damage requiring repair conforms to what, in most orthodox opinions, is the process by which polycyclic hydrocarbons act as carcinogens. The presence of a wide variety of proliferative lesions in the bronchial epithelium that is found, when autopsy is performed on heavy smokers who have died of causes *other* than lung cancer, may have a number of explanations, but by far the simplest is that the lesions are the result of mutational changes giving proliferative advantage to the mutant and its descendants.

Cervical cancer is suspected to be venereal in origin, and herpes virus HS2 is the most likely mediator. If one assumes that HS2 has basically similar reactions to the virus of labial herpes HS1, it is easy enough to devise a hypothesis that would be in line with what is known of herpes virus infections and with the concept of intrinsic mutagenesis. Herpes simplex of the lips is extremely common, but cancer at the site of a recurring lesion there is virtually unknown. The only one I have read of was in an adolescent under continuing immunosuppression for a kidney transplant. It seems that the cell virus interaction in this disease has only two phases. For most of the time the viral genome is in stable association with the somatic cell genome and there are no symptoms; periodically, however, the balance breaks down and the virus multiplies actively and gives the characteristic cell damage and visible blisters. One feature of herpes simplex, however, is the extreme effectiveness of the immune response, which terminates each local outburst with very rapid and complete healing. The possibility exists that minor degrees of activation toward malignancy occur, so that viral antigens appear on the cell surface and rapidly provoke an effective immune elimination of the variant cells. If the cervical mucosal epithelium is not so suitable for immune surveillance, something equivalent to what happened to the lip lesion under continuous immunosuppression could occur. It can be pictured as partial takeover by the viral genome, provoking successful repair of the DNA but introducing informational errors at a much greater than normal rate. The essence of this interpretation of viral action is that damage to host DNA occurs randomly when the standard episomal relation of the viral genome becomes unstable. As such it is entirely analogous to chemical disturbance of DNA structure. Both call for repair by the standard machinery, and, depending on that machinery's degree of error-proneness, informational errors and occasionally cancer will result.

The preceding discussion of the environmental factors in cancer has been absurdly short, and adequate justice has not been done to the much more widely held view that cancer is, for all practical purposes, ascribable to cumulative irritation and damage by environmental carcinogens or viruses. My objective here is simply to show that, given the importance of these environmental factors, the model based on the concept of intrinsic mutagenesis is equally capable of explaining the facts of human cancer, and in addition is applicable to a wide range of other biological phenomena. It is a broad general hypothesis covering events in both structural genes and control DNA, in a general region for which hard experimental data are almost completely lacking. The hypothesis may in fact be very difficult to disprove even in principle, and its claim to be a "good" hypothesis may have to be based only on its heuristic potentiality to lead experimenters to study the phenomena with appropriate techniques from the fields of molecular biology.

Immune Surveillance and Cancer

Any chemical configuration that is not genetically proper to the body can provoke a specific immune response. The existence of idiotypes is perhaps the most striking confirmation of that statement. It is axiomatic to scholars interested in the general pathology of cancer that in most or all cancers the cell membrane differs from the normal state. If these changes are due to somatic mutation, they probably represent either a new peptide configuration or some protein that is different enough from any normal self-pattern to be potentially antigenic. Theoretically, one would expect that under some circumstances immune processes could prevent any overt manifestation of developing tumors.

The evidence that this happens with sufficient regularity to justify giving the process the name of "immunological (immune) surveillance" now appears to be overwhelming. Here I shall mention only those aspects which seem specially relevant to the field I am trying to cover in this book.

For reasons discussed in chapters 3 and 5, the structure of the immune system makes self-monitoring functions to detect and inhibit aberrant lymphocytes both necessary and particularly easy to achieve. It is consistent with this fact that evidence of immune surveillance is most decisive in this field. Positive findings in individuals whose immune system for any reason is functionally deficient are of particular significance. Such findings include any genetic immune deficiency that can, either with the aid of treatment or spontaneously, allow the patient to survive ten years or more; the normal weakening of immune function in old age; and the effect of prolonged treatment with immunosuppressive drugs in patients after kidney transplantation.

The relevant immunodeficiency diseases are agammaglobulinemia, the Wiskott Aldrich syndrome, and ataxia telangiectasia, all of which show lymphoreticular tumors greatly in excess of what would be expected for normal individuals in the same age ranges. In the last two syndromes, many types of malignancy other than lymphomatous conditions may be found. Agammaglobulinemia apparently accompanies only leukemia and lymphoreticular tumors. Good (1970) mentions that individuals with acquired hypoglobulinemia also show a large excess of malignant conditions.

The effect of prolonged therapeutic immunosuppression in producing lymphoreticular malignancies is undoubted; the incidence (in about 1 percent of patients surviving five years) is 350 times what would be expected in a normal population at equivalent ages. Figures show smaller but apparently significant increases in minor forms of neoplasia in skin and cervix uteri, but there is some skepticism about the validity of the observations. Australian surgeons, however, seem convinced that keratoses that would normally remain benign very often develop into squamous epitheliomas on exposed areas of skin in transplant patients under immunosuppression.

The influence on the incidence of lymphoreticular or other forms of cancer by the increase in inefficiency of the immune system with advancing age is controversial. The findings are consistent with the age association of malignant lymphosarcoma, chronic lymphatic leukemia, and the monoclonal gammopathies being determined either by accumulation of somatic mutations or by failure of immune surveillance, and it does not seem possible to find a way of assessing the relative importance of the two processes. One could guess that for these tumors the two factors might be of approximately equal significance. The influence of immune surveillance on epithelial tumors in man is not as well documented. As mentioned earlier, there are genetically based epithelial tumors of the skin that histologically have to be rated malignant but that consistently show self-healing. It is almost inconceivable that this phenomenon is not mediated immunologically, and there is some direct evidence (Brown and Tan, 1973) that immune regression can occur with a third member of the same group, keratoacanthoma. In general, however, the common age-associated types of carcinoma show little evidence that regression can occur, and opinion probably favors the assumption that immune surveillance is an unimportant influence on the age incidence of epithelial tumors.

Finally, we should mention the claim from two investigations that children who have been immunized with BCG against tuberculosis show only 50 percent or fewer cases of acute leukemia in comparison with an unvaccinated population. However, because these were retrospective studies, most commentators feel that until an adequate prospective investigation is organized and followed for a decade, the claim cannot be regarded as proven. But it has not yet been disproven.

The Age Association of Cancer

The general theme of this chapter is that provided we recognize that informational error in DNA of somatic cells can affect both structural genes and the still incompletely understood repetitive DNA with its postulated control function, malignant disease is the accumulation of two or more mutational events in a cell that subsequently gives rise to a proliferating clone of descendent cells.

The striking similarity of the age association of cancer in the two species, mouse and man, at the extreme limits of the range of mammalian lifespans almost demands the conclusion that senescence and cancer are basically the results of a single process—the characteristic rate of somatic mutation in the two species. If this hypothesis is accepted, some interesting consequences follow. First, the common cancers arise from tissues whose cells are subject to the types of mutation that are associated with the manifestations of aging. Second, if error proneness in replication and repair of DNA determines mutation rate and hence average lifespan, the same mechanism must apply to the induction of cancer. Third, in view of the fact that one or more of the mutational events in cancer must involve control DNA, we can deduce that this too is subject to informational error by the same process.

The significance of environmental factors in producing cancer or predisposing someone to cancer is fully established, but the mechanism concerned is controversial. Since all malignant cells transmit all essential qualities to their descendants, the final event that establishes overt malignancy must be concerned with control DNA and take the form of a mutation. This makes us assume, in accord with the general concept of intrinsic mutagenesis, that the effect of the environmental influence is either to damage DNA in such a fashion as to call for increased repair activity or to stimulate normal proliferation, increasing the frequency of DNA replication and of associated errors.

This brings me to the end of my book. Throughout, I have been concerned with the behavior of somatic mammalian cells which, like individuals in a community, have a measure of individuality and freedom and yet are subject to authority and control. One might almost epitomize what I have been saying by regarding the immune system as a purposeful elaboration by evolution of the side of individuality and freedom, and cancer as a pathological escape from control that is in a real sense an accidental but statistically inevitable by-product of another process: i.e., the biological necessity that we and all other mammals must die within some definable lifespan.

I should like to bring together the various topics that I have dealt with by trying to relate them all to the concept of intrinsic mutagenesis, already mentioned at several points. The concept and its implications can be set out in eight brief statements:

1. The fidelity with which a macromolecular pattern in DNA is replicated depends on the molecular structure of the DNA polymerases and other enzymes concerned in the replication.

2. Enzyme structure is determined by structural genes and is therefore subject to the Darwinian process of mutation and survival.

3. The average lifespan of a species is determined by the degree of error proneness of these enzymes, particularly of those influencing the fidelity of DNA reconstruction after damage and repair.

4. The structure of the immune system has required the evolution of a restricted but exceptionally error-prone system to insert unlimited error (diversity) into the variable segments of immunoglobulin.

5. If, as I believe, Baltimore is correct in ascribing most of the generation of diversity to the terminal transferase (see Chapter 2), we can regard that enzyme as a "completely error-prone" derivative of a normal DNA polymerase.

6. A good case can be made for the view that average lifespan in mammals is dependent on the rate of accumulation of genetic errors in somatic cells. It is found, for instance, that in a range of mammalian species, efficiency of DNA repair increases in parallel with average length of life.

7. The characteristic vulnerability of old age as well as a variety of age-associated conditions, including autoimmune disease, amyloidoses, and proliferative diseases of the lymphocyte series, can be ascribed in whole or in part to accumulating errors in the immune system.

8. When a key enzyme of the group handling DNA repair mutates to an exceptionally error-prone form, characteristic disease, of which xeroderma pigmentosum can be taken as a prototype, may result.

9. Finally, as I have discussed in this chapter, the age distribution of cancer in different species can be interpreted as being largely dependent on the degree of error proneness of these same enzymes.

I hope you will recognize that the entire series of discussions in this book has been centered on this concept of intrinsic muta-genesis. It is, I suppose, a heretical concept, but since the early 1970s I have searched, unsuccessfully, for a good reason to discard it. And since I completed the manuscript of the book *Intrinsic Mutagenesis* toward the end of 1973, new discoveries in the relevant fields have all tended to support the concept. Most of them have been incorporated into the foregoing discussions.

REFERENCES

Chapter One

Cole, G. J., and Morris, B. (1971) "The growth and development of lambs thymectomized *in utero.*" *Aust. J. Exp. Biol. Med. Sci.* 49:33–53, and three other related papers, *ibid.* 55–73, 75–88, 89–99.

Marchalonis, J. J. (1975) *Immunity in Evolution.* Harvard University Press, Cambridge, Mass.

Silverstein, A. M., Uhr, J. W., and Kraner, K. L. (1963) "Fetal response to antigenic stimulus. II. Antibody production by the fetal lamb." *J. Exp. Med.* 117:799–812.

Theodor, J. L. (1971) *Thèses.* Faculté des Sciences de Paris.

Chapter Two

Askonas, B. A., Williamson, A. R., and Wright, B. E. G. (1970) "Selection of a single antibody-forming cell clone and its propagation in syngeneic mice." *Proc. Nat. Acad. Sci. USA* 67: 1398–1403.

Baltimore, D. (1974) "Is terminal deoxynucleotidyl transferase a somatic mutagen in lymphocytes?" *Nature* 248:409–411.

Burnet, F. M. (1957) "A modification of Jerne's theory of antibody production using the concept of clonal selection." *Aust. J. Sci.* 20:67–69.

Burnet, F. M. (1967) "The impact of ideas on immunology." *Cold Spring Harbor Symp. Quant. Biol.* 32:1–8.

Eisen, H. N., Little, J. R., Osterland, C. K., and Simms, E. S. (1967) "A myeloma protein with antibody activity." *Cold Spring Harbor Symp. Quant. Biol.* 32:75–81.

Gally, J. A., and Edelman, G. M. (1970) "Somatic translocation of antibody genes." *Nature* 227:341–348.

Hood, L., and Prahl, J. (1971) "The immune system: a model for differentiation in higher organisms." *Adv. Immunol.* 14: 291–351.

Jerne, N. K. (1955) "The natural-selection theory of antibody formation." *Proc. Nat. Acad. Sci. USA* 41:849–857.

Jerne, N. K. (1967) "Summary: Waiting fot the end." *Cold Spring Harbor Symp. Quant. Biol.* 32:591–603.

Jerne, N. K. (1971) "The somatic generation of immune recognition." *Europ. J. Immunol.* 1:1–9.

Kreth, H. W., and Williamson, A. R. (1973) "The extent of diversity of anti-hapten antibodies in inbred mice: anti-NP (4-hydroxy-5-iodo-3-nitro-phenacetyl) antibodies in CBA/H mice." *Europ. J. Immunol.* 3:141–147.

Milstein, C., and Munro, A. J. (1973) "Genetics of immunoglobulins and of the immune response." In H. L. Kornberg and D. C. Phillips, consultant editors, *MTP International Review of Science, Biochemistry—Series One*, Vol. 10 (R. R. Porter, volume editor). University Park Press, Baltimore. Pp. 199–228.

Pauling, L. (1940) "A theory of the structure and process of formation of antibodies." *J. Amer. Chem. Soc.* 62:2643–2657.

Wu, T. T., and Kabat, E. A. (1970) "An analysis of the sequences of the variable regions of Bence Jones proteins and myeloma light chains and their implications for antibody complementarity." *J. Exp. Med.* 132:211–250.

Chapter Three

Burnet, F. M. (1965) "Mast cells in the thymus of NZB mice." *J. Path. Bact.* 89:271–284.

Claman, H. N., Chaperon, E. A., and Triplett, R. F. (1966) "Immunocompetence of transferred thymus-marrow cell combinations." *J. Immunol.* 97:828–832.

Greaves, M. F., Owen, J. J. T., and Raff, M. C. (1973) *T and B Lymphocytes.* Excerpta Medica, Amsterdam, and American Elsevier, New York.

Haustein, D., Marchalonis, J. J., and Crumpton, M. J. (1974) "Immunoglobulin of T lymphoma cells is an integral membrane protein." *Nature* 252:602–603.

Hunt, S. V., and Williams, A. F. (1974) "The origin of cell surface immunoglobulin of marrow-derived and thymus-derived lymphocytes of the rat." *J. Exp. Med.* 139:479–496.

Katz, D. H., Hamaoka, T., Dorf, M. E., and Benacerraf, B. (1973) "Cell interactions between histoincompatible T and B lymphocytes. The H-2 gene complex determines successful physiologic lymphocyte interactions." *Proc. Nat. Acad. Sci. USA* 70: 2624–2628.

Marchalonis, J. J., and Cone, R. E. (1973) "Biochemical and biological characteristics of lymphocyte surface globulin." *Transplant. Rev.* 14:3–49.

Miller, H. R. P., and Jarrett, W. F. H. (1971) "Immune reactions in mucous membranes. I. Intestinal mast cell response during helminth expulsion in the rat." *Immunology* 20:277–288.

Miller, J. F. A. P. (1961) "Immunological function of the thymus." *Lancet* 2:748–749.

Miller, J. J., and Cole, L. J. (1968) "Proliferation of mast cells after antigenic stimulation in adult rats." *Nature* 217:263–264.

Mitchell, G. J., and Miller, J. F. A. P. (1968) "Immunological activity of thymus and thoracic-duct lymphocytes." *Proc. Nat. Acad. Sci. USA* 59:296–303.

Nossal, G. J. V., and Pike, B. L. (1975) "Evidence for the clonal abortion theory of B-lymphocyte tolerance." *J. Exp. Med.* 141:904–917.

Simonsen, M. (1962) "The factor of immunization: clonal selection theory investigated by spleen assays of graft-versus-host reaction." In G. E. W. Wolstenholme and M. P. Cameron, editors, *Ciba Foundation Symposium on Transplantation.* Churchill, London. Pp. 185–209.

Warner, N. L., and Szenberg, A. (1961) "Large lymphocytes and the Simonsen phenomenon." *Nature* 191:920.

Chapter Four

Jerne, N. K. (1971) "The somatic generation of immune recognition." *Europ. J. Immunol.* 1:1–9.

Jerne, N. K. (1976) "The immune system: a web of V domains." (The Harvey Lectures, 1975). Academic Press, New York.

Monod, J. (1972) Chance and Necessity (English translation of *Le Hasard et La Necessité*). Collins, London.

Rowley, D. A., Fitch, F. W., Stuart, F. P., Köhler, H., and Cosenza, H. (1973) "Specific suppression of immune responses." *Science* 181:1133–1141.

Chapter Five

Cleaver, J. E. (1969) "Xeroderma pigmentosum: a human disease in which an initial stage of DNA repair is defective." *Proc. Nat. Acad. Sci. USA* 63:428–435.

Kelner, A. (1949) "Photoreactivation of ultraviolet-irradiated escherichia coli, with special reference to the dose-reduction principle and to ultraviolet-induced mutation." *J. Bact.* 58: 511–522.

Kimura, M. (1968) "Evolutionary rate at the molecular level." *Nature* 217:624–626.

Ohta, T. (1974) "Mutational pressure as the main cause of molecular evolution and polymorphism." *Nature* 252:351–354.

Orgel, L. E. (1963) "The maintenance of the accuracy of protein synthesis and its relevance to ageing." *Proc. Nat. Acad. Sci. USA* 49:517–521.

Report of the Advisory Committee on the Biological Effects of Ionizing Radiations—"The BEIR Report." (1972) National Academy of Sciences, Washington, D.C.

Schekman, R., Weiner, A., and Kornberg, A. (1974) "Multienzyme systems of DNA replication." *Science* 186:987–993.

Watson, J. D. (1970) *Molecular Biology of the Gene*, 2nd edition. Benjamin, Menlo Park, Calif.

Chapter Six

Burch, P. R. J. (1968) *An Inquiry Concerning Growth, Disease and Ageing.* Oliver and Boyd, Edinburgh.

Goodpasture, E. W. (1918) "An anatomical study of senescence in dogs, with especial reference to the relation of cellular changes of age to tumors." *J. Med. Res.* 38:127–190.

Hart, R. W., and Setlow, R. B. (1974) "Correlation between deoxyribonucleic acid excision-repair and life-span in a number of mammalian species." *Proc. Nat. Acad. Sci. USA* 71:2169–2173.

Hayflick, L. (1965) "The limited *in vitro* lifetime of human diploid cell strains." *Exp. Cell Res.* 37:614–636.

Holliday, R., and Tarrant, G. M. (1972) "Altered enzymes in ageing human fibroblasts." *Nature* 238:26–30.

Orgel, L. E. (1963) "The maintenance of the accuracy of protein synthesis and its relevance to ageing." *Proc. Nat. Acad. Sci. USA* 49:517–521.

Walford, R. L. (1969) *The Immunologic Theory of Aging.* Williams and Wilkins, Baltimore.

Williamson, A. R., and Askonas, B. A. (1972) "Senescence of an antibody-forming cell clone." *Nature* 238:337–339.

Chapter Seven

Benditt, E. P., and Benditt, J. M. (1973) "Evidence for a monoclonal origin of human atherosclerotic plaques." *Proc. Nat. Acad. Sci. USA* 70:1753–1756.

Burnet, F. M. (1974) *Intrinsic Mutagenesis.* Medical and Technical Publishing Company, Ltd., Lancaster, England.

Crowe, F. W., Schull, W. J., and Neel, J. V. (1956) *A Clinical, Pathological, and Genetic Study of Multiple Neurofibromatosis.* Thomas, Springfield, Ill.

McKusick, V. A. (1971) *Mendelian Inheritance in Man,* 3rd edition. Johns Hopkins Press, Baltimore.

Nicholls, E. M. (1969) "Somatic variation and multiple neurofibromatosis." *Human Heredity* 19:473–479.

Ohno, S., (1974) "Aneuploidy as a possible means employed by malignant cells to express recessive phenotypes." *In* J. German, editor, *Chromosomes and Cancer.* Wiley, New York. Pp. 77–94.

Orgel, L. E. (1963) "The maintenance of the accuracy of protein synthesis and its relevance to ageing." *Proc. Nat. Acad. Sci. USA* 49:517–521.

Robbins, J. H., et al. (1974) "Xeroderma pigmentosum: an inherited disease with sun sensitivity, multiple cutaneous neoplasms, and abnormal DNA repair." (NIH. Conference). *Ann. Int. Med.* 80:221–248.

Chapter Eight

Burch, P. R. J. (1968) *An Inquiry Concerning Growth, Disease and Ageing.* Oliver and Boyd, Edinburgh.

Jersild, C., Hansen, G. S., Svejgaard, A., Fog, T., Thomsen, M., and Dupont, B. (1973) "Histocompatibility determinants in multiple sclerosis, with special reference to clinical course." *Lancet* 2:1221–1225.

McDevitt, H. O., and Bodmer, W. F. (1974) "HL-A, immune-response genes, and disease." *Lancet* 1:1269–1275.

Maynard Smith, J. (1962) "The causes of ageing." *Proc. Roy. Soc. B* 157:115–127.

Warner, N. L. (1973) "Genetic control of spontaneous and induced anti-erythrocyte autoantibody production in mice." *Clin. Immunol. Immunopath.* 1:353–363.

Chapter Nine

Brown, F. C., and Tan, E. M. (1973) "Immunological reaction in keratoacanthoma, a spontaneously resolving skin tumor." *Cancer Res.* 33:2030–2033.

Burnet, F. M. (1957) "Cancer — a biological approach." *Brit. Med. J.* 1:779–786 and 841–847.

German, J., editor. (1974) *Chromosomes and Cancer.* Wiley, New York.

Good, R. (1970) Discussion *in* R. T. Smith and M. Landy, editors, *Immune Surveillance.* Academic Press, New York. P. 443.

Knudson, A. G., Strong, L. C., and Anderson, D. E. (1973) "Heredity and cancer in man." *In* A. G. Steinberg and A. G. Bearn, editors, *Progress in Medical Genetics,* Vol. 9. Grune and Stratton, New York and London. Pp. 113–158.

Milstein, C., Brownlee, G. G., Cartwright, E. M., Jarvis, J. M., and Proudfoot, N. J. (1974) "Sequence analysis of immunoglobulin light chain messenger RNA." *Nature* 252:354–359.

Proudfoot, N. J., and Brownlee, G. G. (1974) "Sequence at the 3′ end of globin mRNA shows homology with immunoglobulin light chain mRNA." *Nature* 252:359–362.

GLOSSARY

achondroplasia   *genetic disease with shortened limb bones*

agammaglobulinemia   *genetic disease with lack of immuno-globulin*

allergen   *substance provoking allergic disease such as hay fever*

allograft or homograft   *graft from an unrelated animal of the same species*

allotype   *see p. 39*

α-methyl dopa   *drug used to treat hypertension*

ankylosing spondylitis   *rheumatic disease of spine that causes rigidity*

atheroma, atherosclerosis   *forms of arterial disease*

autoradiography   *detection of location of a radioisotope in tissues by allowing it to affect a photographic emulsion*

autosome   *a chromosome other than one of the sex chromosomes*

B cells   *lymphocytes that produce antibody and that are derived from bursa or bone marrow*

Burkitt lymphoma   *malignant disease of African children*

bursa of Fabricius   *organ associated with chicken's lower bowel and source of B cells*

bursectomy   *removal of bursa by hormonal or surgical methods*

carcinoma   *epithelial cancer*

chorioallantoic membrane   *outer living membrane of chick embryo*

clone   *asexually produced descendants of single cell or organism*

complementation   *if two mutant cells both show lack of some function, but, when brought into close relationship by cell fusion, can both manifest it, they are said to show complementation*

cytotoxicity   *capacity to kill or damage cells*

DNA polymerase   *enzyme that helps build up DNA by inserting nucleotide units*

E. coli   *Escherichia coli—a common bacterium widely used in laboratories*

Entwicklungsmechanik   *"mechanism of development" (most of the early work on this subject was published in German)*

eukaryotes   *organisms with visible chromosomes*

fibroblast   *cell common to many tissues and readily cultured*

gammopathy   *disease affecting immunoglobulin of the blood* genome *the genetic mechanism as a whole*

germinal center *accumulation of proliferating cells in the lymph node, spleen, etc.*

Gorgonia *colonial coelenterate with long narrow fronds*

graft-versus-host reaction *damaging effect produced by a graft from another animal on an immunologically ineffective host*

hapten *small molecule responsible for specificity of a complex antigen*

hematopoietic *producing blood cells*

heterozygote *a zygote carrying two different alleles of a given gene*

homeostasis *maintenance of equilibrium conditions in the body*

homozygote *a zygote in which both alleles of the gene are the same*

idiotype *see p. 55*

immunodeficiency disease *a disease due to failure of some immune function*

immunoglobulin *the protein carrying antibody specificity*

immunosuppression *use of drugs to weaken immune response*

karyotype *the number and form of chromosomes in a cell*

lymphokines *soluble substances produced by lymphocytes that can affect other cells*

lymphoreticular tumors *derived from cells related to lymphocytes*

MHCA *major histocompatibility antigen that largely determines the result of transplantation*

macrophage *phagocytic cell with a compact nucleus*

mast cell *granulated cell liberating histamine on stimulation*

mastocytoma *mast cell tumor*

mesenchymal cell *a supporting cell, as contrasted with the specific functional cells of an organ; its many types include fibroblast, macrophage, and lymphocyte*

messenger RNA *the first step in the process of protein synthesis is the transcription of information from DNA to messenger RNA*

monoclonal *referring to a cell population descended from a single cell or to the product, usually immunoglobulin, of such a clone*

monomeric IgM *immunoglobulin M in a single unit contrasting with the normal pentameric form, which is 5 times larger*

NZB (New Zealand Black) mouse *a strain spontaneously showing autoimmune disease*

neoplasia *cancer and other growths*

nucleotides *the units (A, G, C, T or U) from which DNA and RNA are constructed*

phage or bacteriophage *virus that infects bacteria*

phagocyte *cell that takes in and digests bacteria*

phenotype *the bodily appearance of an organism*

plasma cell *B cell derivative that actively produces antibody*

polypeptide *linear chain of amino acids basic to protein structure*

popliteal *situated behind the knee*

postmitotic *a cell that can no longer multiply but continues to function*

purine bases *present in the nucleotides A and G of DNA*

retinoblastoma *cancer of the eye in infants*

somatic *pertaining to body cells, as opposed to germ-line cells*

S—S or disulphide bonds *commonest link by which one peptide chain is attached to another* sterically complementary   *refers to two molecular patterns that fit in a lock-and-key fashion*

T cells   *lymphocytes originating from the thymus*

tandem duplication   *when DNA duplicates abnormally so that the two products are joined end to end and both remain as part of the genome*

thrombocytopenia   *lack of platelets, causing hemorrhages*

thymine dimer   *fusion of two T nucleotide units*

trophoblast   *cells of early embryo specialized to implant the embryo in the wall of the uterus*

zygote   *fertilized ovum from which embryo develops*

INDEX